Ecological Sustainability in Traditional Sámi Beliefs and Rituals

MODERNE
KULTUREN
RELATIONEN

Herausgegeben von Gerhard Droesser und Ruth Hutzel

BAND 20

PETER LANG
EDITION

Mardoeke Boekraad

Ecological Sustainability in Traditional Sámi Beliefs and Rituals

PETER LANG
EDITION

Bibliographic Information published by the Deutsche Nationalbibliothek
The Deutsche Nationalbibliothek lists this publication in the Deutsche Nationalbibliografie; detailed bibliographic data is available in the internet at http://dnb.d-nb.de.

Library of Congress Cataloging-in-Publication Data
Names: Boekraad, Mardoeke, 1964- author.
Title: Ecological sustainability in traditional Sámi beliefs and rituals / Mardoeke Boekraad.
Description: 1 [edition]. | New York : Peter Lang, 2016. | Series: Moderne, Kulturen, Relationen, ISSN 1619-358X ; Band 20 | Includes bibliographical references.
Identifiers: LCCN 2016004131 | ISBN 9783631665985
Subjects: LCSH: Sami (European people)–Religion. | Human ecology–Lapland. | Human ecology–Religious aspects. | Sustainability–Laoland.
Classification: LCC BL980.L3 B64 2016 | DDC 299/.457–dc23 LC record available at http://lccn.loc.gov/2016004131

ISSN 1619-358X
ISBN 978-3-631-66598-5 (Print)
E-ISBN 978-3-653-05893-2 (E-Book)
DOI 10.3726/978-3-653-05893-2

© Peter Lang GmbH
Internationaler Verlag der Wissenschaften
Frankfurt am Main 2016
All rights reserved.
Peter Lang Edition is an Imprint of Peter Lang GmbH.

Peter Lang – Frankfurt am Main · Bern · Bruxelles · New York · Oxford · Warszawa · Wien

This publication has been peer reviewed.

www.peterlang.com

This book is dedicated with gratitude to the Sámi who decided to share their wisdom.

The White Stone won't just find anybody
Only she who wants to search and find,

I, the White Stone, in the shape of a wagtail
Am the truth
I am the envoy of love and hope
My mother Tomorrow's messenger.

From Kirsti Paltto's novel 'The White Stone', 2012.
(translation: by Rauna Kuokkanen and Philipp Burgess)

Preface to the book edition

The publication of this book was made possible by Professor Gerhard Droesser, whose independent view and profound academic knowledge about global ethical issues related to religion I greatly appreciate. It is an immense honor to be proposed to the Peter Lang publishing house by a scholar who has personally experienced and participated in the unfolding moral debates in post-war Germany. His critical and reflective Christian perspective has formed his commitment to the promotion of the highest ethical standards for democracy, tolerance, and ecological sustainability.

This is the book edition of my master's thesis with the same title that was approved in June 2013 by University of Bergen, Norway, Faculty of Humanities' Department of Archeology, History, Cultural Studies and Religion. I could not have completed my master's thesis without the support of Professor Michael Stausberg at Bergen University and the Sámi informants. I am greatly indebted to all persons who agreed to provide information, in particular to Laila Spik and Sigvald Persen. Michael Stausberg gave me invaluable advice and I highly appreciated his critical comments on the draft texts. Marit Myrvoll also provided essential feedback and encouraging words during the research. She has even granted me the utmost privilege of writing an introduction for this publication. The publication was made possible with the financial support of the Umeå University, Institute for Idea and Society Studies, and in particular by the help of Professor Tomas Lindgren. Finally, I need to thank the Norwegian state for their public financing system for students.

The text was completed over two years ago, and the content has not been changed for the book edition. Some minor adjustments and additions were made, in particular in the footnotes. The entire text was linguistically corrected to be ready for publication.

Debates about the theoretical understanding of indigenous religiosity, and, in a wider sense, on how indigenous religiosities have been interpreted by a colonial and hegemonic expression of Christianity, have been increasingly common over the last few years. The study focuses on describing some concrete Sámi beliefs and practices and hopefully is of use for unfolding academic research and debate on these issues, as well as for the Sámi society to reflect upon their own identity. It constitutes an important building block for my current research on the reconciliation process with the Sámi people by the Lutheran Churches of Sweden and Norway. As the discussions on the Anthropocene are becoming increasingly influential, the detailed and partly empirical based knowledge on the way the Sámi relate to ecological sustainability with religious beliefs and rituals might inspire the development of more ecologically sustainable human relationships in all cultures in the world.

Umeå, 1. November 2015.

Introduction to the book edition

This study examines the values, worldviews, perceptions, practices, and the use of nature and natural resources in Sámi relations. Choosing the Sámi people as the subject for her study, Maria Doeke Boekraad aims to give an overview of relevant traditional Sámi myths, beliefs, and rituals and to inquire whether and how they are related to a possibly ecological use of the natural environment. Her study is an important contribution to the thinking and practices of ecological sustainability.

She shows the continuity in the Sámi's practices by referring to written sources and comparing these to her respondents' philosophy on ecological sustainability. As Latour (1993) says, "we have never been modern"; one can extend this to argue that people today are simultaneously traditional/premodern and modern. There is no evidence that the farmer, fisherman, or reindeer herder has changed her/his existential view of the landscape, be it the ocean or the land, despite using modern technology such as motor vehicles, GPS, and navigation radars; to start using modern technology does not necessarily change the basic understanding of oneself and reality. Ingold (2000) argues that the Western academic description of the Western world (to which the Sámi people belong) is of one built on rational thinking in contrast to local understandings that are hard to defend. Ingold says that people in apparently modern societies live their lives by worldviews that have not changed much over time. Therefore, the division between now and then, or tradition or modernity, is frequently wrong.

The author is respectful of her respondents and their wish on one hand that the outside world will get a more realistic understanding of how some Sámi are dealing with local ecosystems and keeping them balanced and usable, and on the other hand the desire to not be romanticized as "ecological saints" who have some type of "perfect" way of dealing with natural resources. The traditional Sámi practitioners are not glorified or stereotyped as "indigenous people living close to nature". On the contrary, Maria Doeke Boekraad manages to give a truthful picture of reflective people not only talking about their ecological philosophy and worldview, but also living it. To support this portrayal, she introduces the reader to the literature on the subject, demonstrating a vast knowledge of former studies and indigenous peoples' sustainable thinking and living worldwide. Her knowledge on written sources concerning Sámi religiosity is truly impressive.

Boekraad also looks at the connection between religious belief and sustainable practices. She examines how traditional thinking and practices still have great value even if there has been a shift in religion. The shift from Sámi religion to Christianity can be looked upon in the same way as Hastrup (1990) explains the change from Norse religion to Christianity in Iceland. The vertical dimension of reality, where the gods live in the upper world, the humans in the middle world, and the dead in the lower world, was quite easily replaced by Christianity's heaven, earth, and hell. Missionaries to the Sámi territory perhaps failed to see, understand, or care about the horizontal dimension of reality – where the fight between cosmos and chaos always takes place. As humans are believed to live in the crossing between the vertical and horizontal dimension, they have to relate to all phenomena that can be a potential threat to human existence and happiness. Therefore, humans have to learn how to deal with these phenomena, such as ogres, animal-mothers (maddu), and underground people. The traditional horizontal model of the cosmos still persists alongside the new model offered by Christianity because there was already a two-dimensional reality (Hastrup 1990: 33).

An example of this is the relation to the underground people. They represent the potential power of chaos, but they can also be helpers as long as humans respect them. To believe in this phenomenon is not contradictory to the belief in Christianity's God – it is more like a belief in neighbors. Everybody knows that neighbors exist even if you do not see them every day. You teach your children to respect them, their property, and their right to exist. Since underground people are unpredictable in their mood and are likely to kidnap your children if you do not pay attention, you have to teach your children how to master such an experience.

Boekraad references an immense volume of written sources, as well as conversations with her participants on their philosophical values that are exemplified through their stories. According to Turner (1986), the story of an experience is always reflexive because the story relates to experience in the past, while at the same time giving expectations of future experiences. Listening to stories to gain insight into people's understanding of reality is thus subject to a double hermeneutics; the researcher interprets what the interpretive actor tells (Geertz 1993 [1973]). Boekraad's methodological choices as well as her excellent command of this method is demonstrated through her work.

Marit Myrvoll, Philosophiae Doctor (PhD), Social Anthropology
September 2015.

Table of Contents

Chapter 1 – Introduction

Ecological Sustainability and Theory of Religion: Sámi Culture as Case Study

In these times of aggravated ecological crises,[1] people throughout the world are reevaluating human values and attitudes toward the physical environment. The so-called large world religions are making efforts to integrate ecological concerns and in offering ways out of the ecological crisis. Environmental education is being integrated into school curricula all over the world (Grim and Tucker 2011). Some important negative trends like the climate change engendered high gas emissions are far from being reversed. The process of understanding how society can create sustainable relationships with the natural environment has not reached its conclusion. Right from the start of the ecological crisis and the ecological movements of the 1960s, indigenous peoples[2] like the Sámi who live in the northern part of Fenno-Scandinavia were being put forward as examples to follow for their supposedly sustainable management strategies (Mathisen 2004). In recent years, this interest shifted to a focus on indigenous knowledge of ecosystems,[3]

---

1 Global climate change, the acidification of the oceans, the massextinction of biodiversity and the spread of dangerous chemicals are amongst those well-documented elements of the crisis which the vast majority of the global scientific community agrees have had an increasing negative impact on the ecosystems which humanity is depending on. Some negative ecological trends have been reversed for instance in terms of harmful ozone emissions, but many have not.

2 The concept of indigenous peoples has become more and more established on both the political and scientific agenda as a result of an international awareness that found its expression via the United Nations. "The international community has not adopted a common definition of indigenous peoples and the prevailing view today is that no formal universal definition is necessaryfor the recognition and protection of their rights. However, there have been attempts to outline the characteristic of indigenous peoples." (UN 2008: 7) See Resource Kit on Indigenous Peoples' issues, by the United Nations' Department for Economic and Social Affairs. For a critical scholary discussion of the term, see. Tafjord 2013.

3 Par. 22: "Indigenous people and their communities and other local communities have a vital role in environmental management and development because of their knowledge and traditional practices. States should recognize and duly support

values and spirituality.[4] The world society is still looking for good examples to follow. I hope to make a useful contribution to that debate through my detailed analysis of Sámi religious traditions with regard to ecological sustainability[5] – but for that, we first need a historical and theoretical framework for the discussion that this introduction hopes to provide.

Primitive Nature

The history of the relationship between European society and indigenous peoples is a complex one and has been characterized by the term "primitivism." Geertz states that primitivism is a philosophical position, which has been a part of all cultures including the European. It consists of paradoxical ideas that one might have regarding indigenous peoples. On the one hand, they are seen as backward and inferior, and on the other hand they are idealized and romanticized. This applies even to science itself. Armin W. Geertz (2004) did an analysis of primitivism where he states that indigenous cultures played a central role in the development of theory in the social and cultural sciences, while at the same time, having been marginalized and even rendered invisible (Geertz 2004: 37). In primitivism, nature becomes a norm for what is good and an ideal for the return to some ideal archaic natural society (Geertz 2004: 41, 55).[6]

---

their identity, culture and interests and enable their effective participation in the achievement of sustainable development" (Rio Declaration on Environment and Development, 12 August 1992).

4 See the declaration of "The Delos 3 Workshop: Diversity of Sacred Lands in Europe," which took place in the Sámi area, in Inari (Lapland), Finland, 1–3 July 2010.

5 Ecological sustainability is defined in the Brundtland report "Our Common Future" (1987) in the following manner: "Sustainable development is development that meets the needs of the present without compromising the ability of future generations to meet their own needs." See also Wu (2013) for an extensive debate about the concept of landscape sustainability science and the definition of ecological sustainability.

6 The suspicion of anti-democratic aspects inherent in the idealization of nature by Green parties and the environmental movement is particularly strong owing to the manner in which the Nazis used social Darwinism in developing their notorious *Blut und Boden* ("Blood and Soil") ideology. This is charactertized by the use of so-called scientific laws of nature to justify the ideol of a "natural"

The myth of the "noble savage" profoundly inspired the European Enlightenment (Geertz 2004: 44). This myth informs a vision of the Sámi, as close to nature and therefore, in particular when Christianized, morally superior to 'civilized' people (Lindmark 2004). In the mid-nineteenth century the ideology of social Darwinism was developed and with it the concept of more and less advanced societies (Lehtola 2004: 44). Indigenous peoples like the Sámi were considered inferior because they were presumed to be at a lower stage of development as compared to others. These normative and discriminatory social Darwinist ideas were considered to be scientific and they influenced state authorities. It was because of this view that a series of discriminatory policies were adopted in all Scandinavian states. Social Darwinist doctrine also inspired fascist regimes and their mass-extermination of "inferior" races before and during the Second World War. After defeat of the fascist armies, the scientific community reacted strongly against this idealization of nature. Together with worldwide decolonization processes, the doctrine of primitivism became outdated in anthropology and other social sciences as well as in the humanities. The fear of a new totalitarian regime based on certain absolute and eternally valid "laws of nature" – combined with a sense of superior racial identity – is still rooted deeply in the European memory. It is therefore understandable that henceforth all movements and intellectual currents which romanticize nature are critically scrutinized for their democratic and humanistic commitment.[7]

But the idealization of nature, the Sámi and other indigenous peoples continues to the present day and takes the form of contemporary neo-primitivism (Geertz 2004, Mathisen 2004). Also the Sámi-inspired neo-shaman movement in Norway idealizes nature and the ancient Sámi religion (Fonneland 2010). Siv Ellen Kraft has analyzed nature-idealizing discourses about the Sámi in which they are represented, according to her, as perfect keepers of the ecological balance (Kraft 2009: 184, 2004: 243).

---

human state of racial purity and its accompanying racial discimination. See Luc Ferry, 1992, "Le nouvel ordre écologique."

7   See Luc Ferry 1992, where the French philosopher draws parallels between the then emergent French Green party and the fascist idealization of natural balances.

The Sámi and other indigenous peoples have become double targets of criticism: as possible source of religious mythologizations of nature and simultaneously as victims of a scientific myth of "natural," for instance social Darwinism when adopted by aggressive regimes.

Some scholars of religion have detected inherent and non-explicit signs of the fact that the ecological movement bears religious traits according to post-secularized concepts of religion. This development was analyzed by the Norwegian scholar of religious studies Tarjei Rønnow (2007: 94–95). Nature in modern Norwegian society, wrote Rønnow (2007: 94), is still considered a source of cultural values, as the model for an ideal society that guarantees a common authenticity, a type of sacred cosmos.[8]

This tendency would seem to carry on to the present day. Internationally we see a group of scientists that even go so far as to declare their positive attitude toward or even full support for "dark green religion," something they see as the last possible resource for changing human societies' attitudes and behavior toward the environment (Taylor 2010, ch. 4 and pp. 220–222).

Geertz is entering a plea for criticism of all forms of anti-humanism and for a "radical revitalization of the Enlightenment project" in order to move beyond such primitivist opinions (2004: 62). Mathisen (2004) claims that if the Sámi should become partners with the ecological movement then they would have to join the discussion solely on the basis of facts. This might also lead to a better understanding of the relationship between indigenous cultures and sustainability – an area which must be addressed by scholars working that common ground shared by the natural and human sciences.

Ecological Saints or Just People like You and Me?

The polemical book *The Ecological Indian* (1999) Shepard Krech III I a strong counterreaction to the depiction of indigenous peoples as "ecological saints" that had emerged in the late 1960s, and was in particular strorgly promoted by Western ecological movements. It was with the help of the natural sciences that analyses were undertaken as to whether specific indigenous

---

8   "I det moderne Norge fremstår naturen som en kulturell verdibank og en projeksjon av det ideelle samfunn. (...) Naturen represener den 'evige lov' og fullkomne orden som er upåvirket av timelighetens omskiftelighet og forgjengelighet. (...) Naturen blir en hellig kosmos" (Rønnow 2007: 94).

cultures really had an ecologically sustainable relationship with their local environments.[9] Some authors like Shepard Krech III focused on examples of indigenous nations that had mismanaged or overused local resources (Krech III 1999). In the Paleolithic era, this might have substantially contributed to extinction of the mammoth and other large and easily caught animals. In recent centuries several American Indian nations did overhunt and exterminate certain animal species (Krech III 1999: passim). In the first book of the geographer and anthropologist Igor Krupnik (1993), on the basis of population calculations of the whale stocks and the caloric needs of the Inuit people, he concluded that they did not have a sustainable way of harvesting whales. According to his observation, Inuit even took pleasure in slaughtering great numbers of whales and were wasting large amounts of whale meat. The Norwegian anthropologist Willerslev, for his part, observed that the Siberian Yukaghir hunting group which he studied in his long-term fieldwork killed every elk that crossed their path. He questioned this practice and the ideas about the dynamics of the elk population which the Yukaghir themselves used as justification for their hunting strategy (Willerslev 2007: 30–34).

Other researchers offered a more nuanced picture of ecologically sustainable behavior and also cited positive cases where biodiversity was strengthened and sustainable balances were kept over a longer period of time. Amazonian indigenous peoples have actively built up highly fertile soils in the Amazon basin and Amazon highlands. They have used these antropogenic soils in agriculture for thousands of years and the soils are essential for their ecologically sustainable agriculture. American students can learn how to maintain and enhance the fertility of the soils through traditional methods that include invoking and communicating with spirits (Apffel-Marglin 2011: 199–202, video).[10] Particularly well elaborated are the studies of the marine scientist Firket Berkes (1999) who examined the "cultural-spiritual complex" as related to the sustainable management

---

9   Along with Shepard Krech III, Diamond and Fikret Berkes are also well known researchers in this field.

10 Explanations by Prof. Apffel-Marglin in the video "Sacred Soil; Revitalizing our Relationship with the Earth and Ending Global Climate Change from Doug Lecomte 2014. https://vimeo.com/91538222 seen on 18. 8. 2015, see also the website of the soil-building projekt Sacha Mama Center in Peru. http://www.casasangapilla.com/sachamamain/ seen on 18.8.2015.

of ecosystems in Canada, and refers to numerous similar studies in other places. Pacific islanders have beliefs and rituals that aim at protecting fragile populations of sea life such as birds and turtles, these including a number of taboos such as the interdiction of hunting during sacred periods along with other rules prohibiting the disturbance of nature (Fikret Berkes 1999/2012: 87). Slash and burn among the Kayapo people in the Asia rainforest increases biological diversity (Fikret Berkes 1999/2012: 75). Australian aboriginals created the pre-European Australian landscape by burning large areas of it in order to keep them inhabited by those species that they relied on for sustenance (Fikret Berkes 1999/2012: 86–87). Some subjects have fomented controversial discussions among biologists, indigenous peoples and anthropologists, like the ecological impact of the Cree's caribou hunt on the caribou population (Fikret Berkes 1999/2012: 95–100 versus Brightman as quoted in Willerslev 2007: 32–33). Berkes' conclusion is that some indigenous cultures manage to maintain ecologically sustainable relations with their ecosystems in certain respects whereas others do not. Traditional cultures are in no way stagnant but, to the contrary, are learning systems based on keen observation of nature and a constant testing of their own ecological concepts as well as on a regular adaption to new circumstances. In some cases, spiritual beliefs are part of a strategy for creating sustainable ecological relations (1999/2012: 86). Berkes describes cases where indigenous peoples have made more thorough observations of nature than biologists, and how this has created conflicts around the subject of nature management with conservationists and state authorities who rely on the authority of scientists. Berkes describes how indigenous peoples place strong value on treating animals with respect in the hunting process (Fikret Berkes 1999/2012: 103).

One can thus conclude that the romanticization of the "Ecological Indian" has been modified in recent decades through international environmental discussions. Indigenous peoples' cultures are now seen as neither more nor less ecologically sustainable than others, even if the terms 'closely related to nature' are often used. Only in specific contemporary cases, they are viewed as making valuable contributions to maintaining ecological sustainability. Efforts to gain a better understanding of individual local practices are an important strategy to gaining a better overall understanding of how ecologically sustainable relations between humans and ecosystems can be conceptualized.

A recent book edited by a representative of the International Union for the Conservation of Nature (IUCN)[11] has gathered many exemplary cases of how local indigenous beliefs and rituals contribute positively to biodiversity and nature conservation in sacred landscapes. The authors conclude that there is an intrinsic link between biological and cultural diversity in sacred landscapes (Verschuuren 2010: 168) and that the spiritual dimension of peoples' relationship with nature must be integrated into nature conservation projects.

Environmental conservation thinking has shifted from a purely quantitative and materialistic approach to a more qualitative view which also takes into account cultural identities of non-western belief systems and spiritual values (Verschuuren 2010: 168).

My thesis is an attempt to realize such a local case study. Its aim is to give an overview of relevant traditional Sámi myths, beliefs and rituals and to inquire as to whether and how they are related to an ecologically sustainable use of the natural environment. The term "ecological sustainability" is linked to emergence of the environmental crisis. Sustainability became part of the international agenda as a result of its use in the 1987 Brundtland report "Our Common Future." (World Commission on Environment and Development 1987).

The idea for this study came from my discussions with Sámi and non-Sámi about environmental issues and Sámi culture. In my opinion, general statements about ecologically sustainable values and attitudes were being regularly made, but there was very little more concrete information about practical Sámi strategies to maintain ecological balances and about the role that religious beliefs and practices played. During my research it turned out that there were few analytic sources which had addressed ecological issues under the angle of sustainability. Therefore it seemed that the most logical choice approach was to create a kind of inventory, to undertake a broad and comprehensive study rather than focusing on one specific belief, ritualistic element or locality. This study hopes to be able to provide information that

---

11 "Founded in 1948 as the world's first global environmental organization. Today the largest professional global conservation network. A leading authority on the environment and sustainable development." (From www.iucn.org/about, read on 18. aug. 2015).

can contribute to a more nuanced debate about Sámi identity and sustainability.

In order to achieve this aim, first a choice had to be made as to the relevant materials. The information we have about Sámi religious relationships with ecosystems comes mostly from the Sámi pre-Christian tradition, even if in recent times some Christian elements have joined in (Johnsen 2005). The available information starts with secondary sources like ancient missionary texts from the time of the religious change in the seventeenth and eighteenth centuries. The first written primary sources date from the end of the twentieth century. These sources will be complemented with findings derived from my own interviews.

One important limitation of this study is that I could not verify the factual ecological sustainability of the Sámi's local ecosystems. For instance I did not find general overviews of the ecological development of inland fishing lakes or coastal bird islands over longer periods. It is therefore impossible to verify the biological truth of informants' statements describing their ecologically sustainable management of specific locales. As biologist myself, I believe that their information is in many cases most likely accurate in terms of the fish populations, bird islands, game, local forests and berry fields, because of documentation showing that the same lakes and islands have been in continuous use over long periods by the same communities and families. From this can be concluded that the system must have been effective at most places.[12] The methodological choices of the research are explained in greater detail in chapter 2.

Indigenous People's Religion and the Link to the Land

The link to the land is considered a key aspect to ecological sustainability, as indigenous peoples see themselves as responsible for the lands they inhabit. This is expressed in the United Nations' Declaration On The Rights Of Indigenous Peoples:

---

12 One quantitative study on sustainable landscape management appeared after the publication of the study confirms that the pre-industrial use of key-specie Scots pine by Sámi peoples and farmers in Pite Lappmark, a surface of 20 759 square km, was ecologically sustainable from 1550 to 1910 (Rautio, Josefsson, Axelsson & Östlund 2015).

Art. 25: Indigenous peoples have the right to maintain and strengthen their distinctive spiritual relationship with the traditionally owned or otherwise occupied and used lands, territories, waters and coastal seas and other resources and to uphold their responsibilities to future generations in this regard (United Nations Declaration On The Rights Of Indigenous Peoples, adopted on 7 July 2007).

Ecological sustainability is not explicitly mentioned or addressed in article 25. It is somehow supposed to be an inherent part of the "distinctive spiritual relationship" with the ecosystems that they owned or lived on and that there exists a responsibility toward future generations. This type of declaration reflects nothing more than intentions. The statement does not refer to a need for a global sustainable strategy, as it only refers to lands that are owned or used by indigenous peoples. This article refers to a value system of sustainability and it testifies the acknowledgment of human's relationship to physical reality. The sustainability paragraph is closely followed by the claim on control of certain landareas. The following article includes this phrase:

Indigenous peoples have the right to own, use, develop and control the lands, territories and resources that they possess by reason of traditional ownership or other traditional occupation or use, as well as those which they have otherwise acquired. United Nations Declaration On The Rights Of Indigenous Peoples art. 26.2, adopted on 7 July 2007.

The claim of owning or controlling lands is central to the declaration, not the sustainable management of it or of the planet as a whole.

The Dutch scholar of religion J. G. Platvoet has described the main features of African tribal religions. The first is locality and non-expansionism, the second is the centrality of kinship – meaning the link with ancestors and animals too seen as kin – and the third characteristic is the transmission via oral traditions (quoted by Cox 2007: 61–63).

Indigenous people define themselves as connected, as being part of the lands they inhabit. They often say that they desire the right to use them as they wish. The link to the land is mostly defined in spiritual terms and has resulted in direct political implications such as claiming land rights and right of exclusive use regarding the natural resources. Many indigenous peoples or at least important parts of their population wish to continue, also in the modern context, nature-related traditional lifestyles and economic activities like hunting and fishing, while at the same time wishing to be part of the modern globalized modern. International public opinion is regularly mobilized[13] to support indigenous peoples in their protests against all sorts of large-scale ecologically devastating projects that threaten traditional indigenous lifestyles, like hydroelectric plants, oil exploitation in rainforests, extraction of oil sand in Canada, and so on. Many nations are mobilized to protect their traditional economies and lifestyle. The international declarations do not necessarily have a direct and coherent consequence for practical action with regard to sustainability, but they emphasize the importance of a sustainable value system that is bound to locality.

Definition of Terms related to Religious Expressions

In order to describe the beliefs and rituals, it is first necessary to provide a theoretical framework of the concepts and terms to be used. Beliefs and rituals are as aspects of human culture that play a number of roles in social, psychological and ecological terms. Various branches of the modern sciences are presently trying to give better explanations of what religious belief and rituals consist of and just how they function.

There is no unanimous definition of religion. There has been an important critique by scholars on what they perceive as onesided and biased 'Western' 'Protestant', Christian- or 'liberal' definition of terms like 'religion' and 'secular. (Talal Asad 2003).

A basic definition of religion is formulated by Gilhus and Mikaelsson:

> a relationship to a universe of beliefs and concepts that is characterized by communication about and with hypothetical gods and powers (Gilhus and Mikaelsson 2001: 29, my translation).[14]

For my research I will rely upon certain aspects of the following three definitions of religion as a basis. The important element is that religion consists of relationships and communication that are also important in my research. The communication takes place with "hypothetical" gods and powers. "Hypothetical" implies that whether humans believe in those gods

---

13 For instance by the international action groups Cultural Survival and Survival International.
14 "Religion er menneskers forhold til forestillingsunivers som kjennetegnes av kommunikasjon om og med hypotetiske guder og makter" (Gilhus & Mikaelsson 2001: 29).

and powers is not primarily relevant. The term of "powers" to designate superhuman agents is found in many sources on religion and also appears to be used by the informants of other researchers.

The word "god" is culturally biased in relation to the European religious traditions; a more neutral and universal term might be that proposed by cognitive science of religion, namely "superhuman agents" (Lawson & McCauley 1990).

The second definition of collective "superhuman agents," according to Lawson and McCauley, is embedded in their work on the cognitive science of religion and attempts to link religious elements to objective, universal and experimentally measurable and testable cognitive mechanisms:

> We construe a religion as a symbolic-cultural system of ritual acts accompanied by an extensive and largely shared conceptual scheme that includes culturally postulated superhuman agents (Lawson & McCauley 1990: 5).

Here is the observable element of religion – the ritual expression – which is also regarded as its central characteristic. The superhuman agents are the acting entities in rituals. They are seen as having more than human power, as being special in some certain sense.

As can be seen in this discussion of definitions, it is not easy to find terms that are universally applicable in describing religious expressions. Words like "god," "symbol" or "supernatural agent" have been debated in the academic discourse. In a recent issue of the Norwegian magazine for religious studies, Håkon Tandberg summarizes the international debate on this (2013: 13–15). One of the terms proposed by the cognitive scientist P. Boyer is "counterintui-tive agents" – counterintuitive because superhuman agents act in "miracu-lous" ways that go against what one expects as regular behavior, for instance a ghost that walks though a wall. The term "superhuman" was first proposed by Melford Spiro (1966). It refers to beings with greater powers than those that are given to humans. The "super" powers originate from the cultural heritage of the social group (Tandberg 2013: 14), which links the term to the social functioning of religion. Tandberg concludes that this term is neutral and descriptive and therefore best suited for use in research and religious sci-ence. I join him in that conclusion. The word does not have significance or connotations in our cultural context. This is an advantage because it is not connected to the normative world of any existing religious tradition. It is still somehow recognizable as having something to do with beliefs and rituals.

The two missing factors in these definitions are the role of elements that are not superhuman agents but symbols as well as the role of religion in structuring existence and in creating motivations and meaning. These elements we can find in the classic definition of Clifford Geertz, the influential American cultural anthropologist:

> Religion is: (1) a system of symbols which acts to (2) establish powerful, pervasive, and long-lasting moods and motivations in men by (3) formulating conceptions of a general order of existence and (4) clothing these conceptions with such an aura of factuality that (5) the moods and motivations seem uniquely realistic (Geertz 1985, original 1966: 4).

In my view the characteristics and patterns of the relationship with ecosystems are included in the term cultural system, as our attitudes to nature and ecology are culturally determined.

It is with these definitions of the last decades that the study of religion has taken a large step forward. Religion is no longer seen as being the exclusive domain of some formalized group with a coherent doctrine and directed by religious virtuosos but as consisting of a series of religious functions and expressions that are part of overall social functioning. Its aim is to give meaning to human existence. It can mobilize people for ideals, for instance through societal movements like for instance some forms of religiously inspired environmentalism (Rønnow 2007: 95, referring to Talal Asad and James A. Beckford).

Even if I study religious beliefs and rituals, I have decided to avoid the term "Sámi religion" in this text because it has an immediate association with the ancient and now extinct pre-Christian religion.

The concept of "folk beliefs" will not be used in this work because it is seen as the expression of a hierarchy between an elite or authorized group and "the masses" (Pyysiäinen 2004: 160).

Håkan Rydving argues that the concept of folk religion has had common currency since the Enlightenment period when certain remains of pre-Christian religions were designated superstition and folk beliefs (Rydving 2004: 143). The concept of folk religion served to highlight those non-official beliefs that otherwise could have easily been neglected. This is different at present – scholars can simply study Sámi religion in all its diverse aspects (Rydving 2004: 148).

Rituals hold a central place in the study of religion for various reasons. First, they are objectively observable and a good object of investigation. They are also recognized as a "universal medium of symbolic expression," even if Bell sees the term of ritual as a cultural and historical construction by worldwide academia (Bell 1997: 1, 262). Ritual structures reinterpret our world, create and renew community, transform individual identity and provide meaning through the confirmation of human identity as situated in the cosmos (Bell 1997: 264, 266). Ritual incorporates the physical experience of symbols and beliefs as a practical-based action (Bell 1997: 1, 266, 1992: ix); rituals construct authority and power relations (1997: 82).

A. Irving Hallowell developed the concept of non-human personhood in his study of the Native American nation of the Ojibwe (1960/2002). He describes the way in which objects are seen as animated and acquire the attribution of personhood. Some authors propose psychological explanations for the projection of personhood to such things as stones and animals. Willerslev establishes a reasoning linked to mimetic practices in which non-human personhood allows a double perspective of identification creating boundaries with animals and the like in an overall logic of relationality (Willerslev 2007).

The concept of non-human personhood has led to an attempt to rehabilitate and revitalize the concept of animism, in particular by the English scholar Graham Harvey (2006). Harvey has been criticized for having a pro-animist theological agenda, for giving an apologetic and idealized version of how harmonious and beneficent the relations between the non-human persons in a system of animism must be (Cox 2007: 65). Armin Geertz considers animism to be a term often associated with totemism, still too often linked to primitivism, and he advices its avoidance (2007: 340). Yet many scholars have adopted the concept of animism in describing belief systems (e.g. Brightman, Grotti and Ulturgasheva 2012). A recent study by Willerslev (2007) uses the concept of animism in a non-pejorative sense to show how violent the relations with non-human persons can be. He describes how a hunter can be tricked into death (2007: 68, 82); how spirits are able to "colonize" each other mentally (2007: 50) and how hunters can sexually attract elks by spiritual and physical means to make them come close enough to be killed (2007: 76, 87, 104–105, 110). Willerslev criticizes scholars like Durkheim for treating indigenous peoples as intellectually inferior and pretending that these peoples would not themselves have understood the nature of their animist beliefs. Could Western scholars only understand those beliefs by developing models of psychological projections? For the Siberian people of the Yukaghirs there is a sole reality in which human and non-human persons have relationships.

Willerslev has recorded that the Yukaghir were convinced that spirits are found in the world and, at the same time, that they are constructed by human cultural patterns. Willerslev gives more detailed descriptions of the ways Yukaghir perceive the spirits, but it is not necessary to go into more details here (Willerslev 2007: 185).

In addition, and in concordance with the topic of this thesis, there is the question of how religious systems contribute to establishing a structured and meaningful relationship with the natural environment. In order to establish a contact with the environment in the first place, the significance of the material existence of the human body has to be understood. McGuire argues that after the Reformation the Catholic and Protestant churches attempted to expunge from religion all references to the body, seeing it as impure (McGuire 2008: 55). In recent decades scholars of religion have been reassessing the reality of that supposed disconnect between human mind and body. Humans not only have a mind but a body and the two cannot be seen as totally separate from each other. In the opinion of Merleau-Ponty, a theoretical perspective on human consciousness is impossible without embodiment (McGuire 2008: 113). McGuire emphasizes that the material (especially the bodily) aspects of popular religious practice are important parts of how the larger religious experience is produced (McGuire 2008: 56). Physical experiences like hunger, pain, sickness, childbirth, and death are key themes in religious expressions. There is no dualistic distinction between aspects that are "purely" spiritual and those that are "merely" physical and material (McGuire 2008: 56).

As part of this tendency, a number of theories about the importance of emplacement have been developed. They see religious expression as necessarily locative by providing meaning to places and binding people to a location (Tweed quoted in Hughes 2012: 13). For instance, a cult can continue even if the population no longer inhabits the place it is linked to. The Cubans in exile in Florida still venerate the Catholic Madonna who is the patroness of Cuba (Tweed quoted in Hughes 2012: 210). Religion can divide space and create boundaries, so that some places become carriers of certain meanings while others are not (Rappaport 1999: 209–215).

Religion as Creating a Relationship with the Natural Environment

Religious expressions not only create a relationship between people but between people and their physical environment. As such, they create values, attitudes and beliefs that concern the human environment, be it animals, plants or stones. Roy Rappaport, an American anthropologist (1926–1997), researched in detail how local rituals create a "delicate but essential environmental balance" (Bell 1997: 29). He did field work among the Papua people of the Tsembaga Maring and looked at how they kept a balance between people, the gardens and the pigs by making a ritual of their mass slaughtering – the ritual itself was the regulating factor and not only its symbolic expression (Rappaport 1975: 3). Rappaport counted the pigs, the amount of land required, and the estimated crop yields in order to prove his hypothesis convincingly. Rappaport has been called a neo-functionalist (Segal 2012: 69, Bell 1997: 29) because he assigns a central role to religion in creating a balanced human society. In his last book, Rappaport suggests that the entire humanity should start using religions to create harmonious bonds between humans and their non-human environments (Rappaport 1999). Here he is clearly going beyond his role as scientist and becoming theological.

As to the way the thesis is organized, here follows an overview of the chapters. After this introductory chapter, I will explain the methodologies of the research, the perspective I have adopted as well as the criteria for selection of information sources and informants and I will also be describing the properties of these sources. In the chapter to follow, I will present brief surveys of the Sámi's cultural, historical and ecological background of the Sámi will be given, and I will explain the term "traditional Sámi culture." It will also be explained how the concept of ecological sustainability fits into the Sámi world-view and how some Sámi themselves think about their culture's postwar development with respect to sustainability. In the next four "mapping" chapters, the actual beliefs, rituals and also stories that function as myths will be systematically described and analyzed. The approach is spatial and goes from the individual entity to the species-related, the local, the regional and up to the universal level. At the end I will draw my conclusions.

It must also be said that this study is not intended to be comparative. I will limit myself to inquiring into Sámi views of religion, nature and animals without raising the question as to whether they are substantially different from the local Fenno-Scandinavian people of, say, 50, 150 or 500 years ago. Many of the superhuman agents here described are present in the neighboring cultures and have at first glance very similar looking functions. It is not my intention to show that the Sámi are now or were once in the past more sustainable than other neighboring peoples. A comparative approach was beyond the parameters of this research.

Chapter 2 – Sources and Methodology

In this chapter my methodology, my perspective and the used sources will be discussed. The starting point of this study was my encounter with a number of traditional practices, some of which have partly disappeared but are recalled by elderly persons, some are just practiced by a few persons, while others are still in general use. I tried to find out more about their spread and to trace them back in time. In that research process I uncovered ever more new information, some of which was unexpected.

Obviously it is impossible to read every source that exists about particular local elements of Sámi religion and, because of that, I decided to limit my selection to the best known primary sources, to oral traditions written down by Sámi in recent decades, and to my own interviews. In the interviews I was trying to test the information I found in various texts and to find more relevant elements.

While I recognize that there are differences between the various regions, I covered all of them because most beliefs and rituals are represented in several areas. However a special focus is on the Northern Sámi, being the largest region and also for me the most easily accessible one because of my personal background. All my informants are Northern Sámi, while one of them, Laila Spik, is both Northern and Lule Sámi. I use information from T. I. Itkonen about the Inari Sámi, and I will compare traditions when the sources allow for this. For every religious element I describe, the regional provenance is indicated as precisely as possible. The combination of ancient sources and interviews corresponds to what a number of Sámi scholars such as Marit Myrvoll or Nils A. Oskal have done in their description of Sámi value and belief systems.[15] They connect contemporary beliefs and rituals to ancient ones, some of which had been described by missionaries, while others had not.

---

15 See Marit Myroll (2010) and her analysis of a local Lule-Sámi village in Nordland, Norway; Nils A. Oskal's study of the values of Western Finnmark reindeer herding (1995); Magga, Oskal and Sara (2001) and their contribution to the ethics of animal welfare; and Jorunn Jernsletten in her research in Norwegian Southern Sámi areas on the relationship to the landscape (2002, 2004).

Of course one can never be sure about the historic dimension of a value, belief or ritual that has been described in the last fifty or hundred years in the missionary accounts or other written sources. It is not the aim of this study to reconstruct some kind of authentic ancient Sámi religion; it is sufficient to describe traditional local cultures that have probably existed for at least the last 200 years. Still I believe that these type of long-term connections are important to make, as it is also possible that oral traditions might be of more ancient provenance.

2.1 Indigenous Methodologies[16]

Indigenous peoples all over the world are undergoing a process called decolonization (Tuhiwai 1999, Kuokkanen 2000) and reflecting a wish to ascend to their rightful social and cultural positions and thus obtain more control over their own society and culture. This often creates a dichotomy with what they call "Western science," which follows its own agenda and tends to disregard the concerns of the people under study while often misunderstanding their indigenous beliefs (Tahuwai Smith 1999: 74, Kuokkanen 2000).

> The values, attitudes, concepts and language embedded in beliefs about spirituality represent, in many cases, the clearest contrasts and between indigenous peoples and the West. These are among the few aspects of ourselves which the West cannot decipher, cannot understand and cannot control … yet (Tuhiwai Smith 1999: 74).

Also in Sámi sources we find frequent remarks that non-Sámi do not understand or should not be told things so that the Sámi will not be considered as idiots. Turi speaks of how he cannot disclose all about traditional medicine because it might not be believed and could even be seen as ludicrous:

> For many learned men it is not suitable to hear all this advice. They do not believe in it and just ridicule the Sámi's foolishness; but if they really acquainted themselves with all that the Sámi do, they would be surprised with the amount of their power and where it comes from (Turi 2012/1910: 123).[17]

---

16 The Sámi University College in Kautokeino has published an English version of the report of the seminar "Ethics in Sámi and Indigenous Research," which took place in Karasjok on 23–24 October 2006, in the Dieđut Series 1/2008.

17 "(…) og for mange lærde herrer passer det ikke å høre om alle rådene. De tror ikke på dem, de gjør bare narr av samens dumhet, men om de fikk se alt hva

Pehr Fjellström (b. 1697), the Swedish priest (who worked in the Lycksele and the Pite Sámi area) wrote that even after the forty years that he spent as a priest with the Sámi, the Sámi kept all things related to their ancient religious practice a secret (1755/1981: 13). And contemporary researchers of religion might still encounter the same attitude, in all parts of the world, one example being from Central America in Tafjord in Natvig (2006: 250).

In order to create good relations, several protocols for research on indigenous cultures have been conceived for outside researchers.[18] Socials scientists are developing creative new practices, calling for critical research, for qualitative or participatory action research, for working with indigenous communities to make sure that the local community is committed to the research and sees the benefits of it (Denzin, Lincoln & Tuhiwai Smith 2008: 9). The personal investment of the researcher is central; some scholars propose that he or she could become auto-ethnographic and undergo a personal transformative process that generates postcolonial moments of knowledge transformation (Tomaselli, Dyll & Francis 2008: 368, Helander–Renvall 2009: 46). Indigenous methodologies are based on ethnic borders and indigenous/non indigenous power sharing. For my research, the following points are relevant: the research question should concern issues that are put forward by the indigenous peoples themselves, the results should be made available to them in a way that strengthens the indigenous society, and research by persons with an inside perspective should be strongly developed (Tuhiwai Smith 1999, Porsanger 2004).

My study tries thererfore to adopt some certain principles of the indigenous methodologies. Even if not a Sámi myself, it is possible to have some inside knowledge of Sámi society. Both aspects will be combined – to be an understanding, neutral observer who is supportive of the Sámi culture and being a reflexive and critical outsider (Porsanger 2005: 27–31). The subject of my research has been developed in dialogue with various Sámi who have an environmental concern, such as ecological activists. The three

---

samer gjør, så skulle de forundre seg over denne makta, og hvor den kommer fra" (Turi 2010/1910: 123).

18 See for instance "Negotiating Research Relationships: A Guide for Communities," www.arbediehtu.no, Sámi University College, Kautokeino, and Kuokkanen, 2009, pp. 132–144.

key informants – who are unacquainted and live in separate communities – have clearly expressed that they wished on the one hand that the outside world had a more realistic understanding of how some Sámi dealt with the local ecosystems to keep them balanced and usable, and that on the other hand they did not wish to be romanticized as "ecological saints" who have some kind of "perfect" way of dealing with natural resources. They merely seek to provide a differentiated way of showing how the traditional Sámi culture with which they grew up is based on life experience. I am grateful that Marit Myrvoll, an experienced researcher and Sámi social anthropologist, has made herself available to discuss these themes on several occasions and to offer her comments regarding my outlines. This project has been accepted and registered at the Norwegian Social Science Data Services. My supervisor Professor Michael Stausberg (University of Bergen) has helped me enormously. The Department of Archaeology, History, Cultural Studies and Religion of the University of Bergen was so kind to contribute with a travel grant. Allegra Brunborg offered invaluable assistance in correcting my English for the master's thesis text.

2.2 My Perspective as Researcher

My research perspective is composed of several experiences and aims. As a biologist and life-long environmental activist I wish to contribute to finding solutions for the global ecological crisis. Feeling part of Sámi society myself, I wish to strengthen Sámi culture and create greater knowledge, awareness and debate about Sámi cultural values. Last but not least I am a scholar and seek to foster a more informed debate about the Sámi relationship to ecological sustainability.

I have lived several years with a militant and traditionally minded Sámi and am parent of our Sámi child. Together we inhabited a local village community in Eastern Finnmark where I took active part in local Sámi society and initiated and coordinated cultural projects on both the local and international level.[19]

---

19 Here are three examples that had tangible results: the Deanu Salmon Seminar in 2003, led by the University of Rovaniemi; the making of a cultural trail and a brochure in the village of Sirma, in cooperation with the local inhabitants' association Sirma bygdelag, in 2007; and with Niiillas A. Somby, 2008, the

I also learned the Northern Sámi language at an avanced level. Over the years I have acquired cultural knowledge of the Sámi and personally identify with their society. My perspective has become mixed, being partly outsider and partly insider – an insider because I have knowledge of the culture from personal experience, being part of a Sámi family and local community, and an outsider because I am also part of non-Sámi cultures.

In my view it is difficult to see the inside and outside perspectives as absolutely dichotomous because they can frequently overlap (Porsanger 2004: 27–28). An outsider might gain knowledge rapidly whereas an insider perspective is no guarantee for accountability; there is a great variety of insider views (Porsanger 2004: 109).

In my opinion, research from all perspectives is equally authoritative and important – each perspective has its various advantages and disadvantages. The discussion and exchange between research made from different perspectives is of crucial importance for creating a fertile and creative scientific life.

2.3 Types of Sources

The discussion of the value and reliability of the sources that provide knowledge about ancient Sámi beliefs and rituals is a traditional item of recent texts about Sámi religiosity (Bäckman 1975, Mebius 2007, Porsanger 2007). Sources for gathering information are generally differentiated into verbal or non-verbal, and primary or secondary. Verbal sources are texts or linguistic terminology and (place) names, while non-verbal sources consist of objects such as sacred drums, graves or sacred and archeological sites. Primary sources represent insider views, they are direct and unchanged data, whereas in a secondary source the direct information has already been transformed by an outsider's selection, interpretation or reformulation (Rydving 1993: 27–42, 2010: 8, Porsanger 2007: 73–85).

Sources about Sámi religious practices can be traced back to the earliest written sources available about pre-Christian religion to texts from the missionaries in the seventeenth and eighteenth centuries (i.e. secondary sources). As previous scholars have not explicitly focused on the subject I was looking

---

video documentary *Sámi Traditional Knowledge About the Use of Nature*, see note in chapter 3.

at – the relationship between religion and sustainability – I often had to look for marginal observations in longer texts.

According to Jelena Porsanger, a scholar in religious studies at the Sámi high school who researched and analyzed the sources for the indigenous religion of the Eastern Sámi (Porsanger 2007), the use of contemporary primary oral courses was at first contested by scholars who considered the ancient religion to have disappeared. Any potential remaining signs of "folk" religion were seen as lacking their original context and had therefore become irrelevant. But thereafter it became common practice for scholars to construct historical continuities between beliefs and rituals of the nineteenth and twentieth centuries and even earlier (see scholars such as Laura Honko and Juha Pentikäinen and later Hans Mebius 1972 quoted in Porsanger 2007: 75–76).[20]

Porsanger includes interviews with contemporary Eastern Sámi as a valid primary source for Skolt Sámi ancient traditional religious traditions (2007: 80, 83). Louise Bäckman remained careful and skeptical in pointing to changes in oral traditions and significant variations between, for instance, what a *noaidi*[21] and ordinary people said (Porsanger 2007: 76–77). Factors that cause changes in narratives transmitted via oral traditions have been little researched and every source must be evaluated for its individual quality.

The religious elements described in this study are stated to be traditional and inherited by means of narratives stemming from oral transmission by primary sources like Johan Turi, who was born around 1850, or the persons who wrote down the stories for K. J. Qvigstad around 1880.

In this chapter my methodology and perspective and sources will be discussed. The starting point of this study was my encounter with a number of traditional practices, some of which have partly disappeared but are recalled by elderly persons, some are just practiced by a few persons, while others are still in general use. I tried to find out more about their spread and to

---

20 Mebius even refers to a likely continuity of orally transmitted traditions recorded in the twentieth century until the seventeenth century (quoted in Porsanger 2006: 75).
21 The Noaide was the religious expert or virtuoso of the ancient Sámi religion. The term is extensively described in Mebius 2007, and the terms for the noaide, by Rydving (2010: 73–92).

trace them back in time. In that research process I uncovered ever more new information, some of which was totally unexpected.

Obviously it is impossible to read every source that exists about particular local elements of Sámi religion and, because of that, I decided to limit my selection to the best known primary sources, to oral traditions written down by Sámi in recent decades, and to my own interviews. In the interviews, I was trying to test the information I found in various texts and to find more relevant elements.

While I recognize that there are differences between the various regions, I covered several of them because most beliefs and rituals are represented in different areas. However, a special focus is on the Northern Sámi, being the largest region and also for me the most easily accessible one because of my personal background. All my informants are Northern Sámi, while one of them, Laila Spik, is both Northern and Lule Sámi. I use information from T. I. Itkonen about the Inari Sámi, and I will compare traditions when the sources allow for this. For every religious element I describe, the regional provenance is indicated as precisely as possible.

The combination of ancient sources and interviews corresponds to what a number of Sámi scholars such as Marit Myrvoll or Nils A. Oskal have done in their description of Sámi value and belief systems.[22] They connect contemporary beliefs and rituals to ancient ones, some of which had been described by missionaries, while others had not.

Of course one can never be sure about the historic dimension of a value, belief or ritual that has been described in the last fifty or hundred years in the missionary accounts or other written sources. It is not the aim of this study to reconstruct some kind of authentic ancient Sámi religion; it is sufficient to describe traditional local cultures that have probably existed for at least the last two hundred years. Still I believe that these type of long-term connections are important to make, as the possibility that that oral traditions might be of very ancient provenance can not be excluded.

---

22 See Marit Myroll (2010) and her analysis of a local Lule-Sámi village in Nordland, Norway; Nils A. Oskal's study of the values of Western Finnmark reindeer herding (1995); Magga, Oskal and Sara (2001) and their contribution to the ethics of animal welfare; and Jorunn Jernsletten in her research in Norwegian Southern Sámi areas on the relationship to the landscape (2002, 2004).

On Oral Primary Sources

Oral primary sources are recordings or written records of oral living traditions that are captured in an authentic manner, that means, with the intention to be respectfull to the tradition and to make as little changes in the content as possible. The value of these sources how stable and ancient they are and could testify about pre-Christian ancient Sámi religious practices has been a frequent topic for scholarly discussion. According to Jelena Porsanger, the use of contemporary primary oral courses was at first contested by scholars who considered the ancient religion to have disappeared and any potential remaining signs of "folk" religion as lacking their original context and therefore irrelevant. But thereafter it became common practice for scholars to construct historical continuities between beliefs and rituals of the nineteenth and twentieth centuries (see scholars such as Laura Honko and Juha Pentikäinen and later Hans Mebius 1972 quoted in Porsanger 2007: 75–76).

Porsanger includes interviews with contemporary Eastern Sámi as a valid primary source for Skolt Sámi ancient traditional religious traditions (2007: 80, 83). Louise Bäckman remained careful and skeptical in pointing to changes in oral traditions and significant variations between, for instance, what a *noaidi*[23] and ordinary people said (Porsanger 2007: 76–77). According to general opinion, factors that cause changes in narratives transmitted via oral traditions have been little researched and every source must be evaluated for its individual quality.

The religious elements described in this study are stated to be traditional and inherited from their ancestors by the first primary informants like Johan Turi who were born around 1850. To make a rapid and maybe superficial evaluation of the datation of an oral tradition that was for the first time recorded in the late nineteenth century, it cannot be claimed with absolute certainty that any oral tradition existed previous to about 1750. It can be supposed that if Johan Turi had heard about a tradition from his grandparents, then they probably told him what they themselves had heard from their great

---

23 *Noaide* was the religious expert or virtuoso of the ancient Sámi religion. The term is extensively described in Mebius 2007, and the terms for the *noaide*, by Rydving (2010: 73–92).

or great-great grandparents, i.e. those born circa one hundred years earlier, around the midle of the eithteenth century, which was the period when in some areas the ancient religion could not be practiced any more in public (Rydving 1993). Any claims of longer chains of memory are in my opinion rather difficult to prove without supplementary evidence.

After the Second World War, and in particular over the last four decades, academic traditions changed and many scholars started recording primary sources. Also theologians treated Sámi culture in more a respectfull manner. Examples are the finnish Sámi minister Nilla Outakoski and recent studies on nature theology by northern Sámi theologian Tore Johnsen who then was minister in the local congregation The southern Sámi minister Bierna Bientie (2003) has written important texts on Sámi nature-related religiosity. University centers in Tromsø, Kautokeino, Oulu, Helsinki, Åbo, Uppsala, Umeå and others have built up expertise on Sámi religiosity. Sámi scholars claimed their Sámi ethnicity and started describing and analyzing their culture from inside perspectives. The theme of traditional religiosity as related to the landscape and nature has attracted increasing interest.[24]

Ancient Written Sources

Much has been written about the available sources of information regarding pre-Christian religions. We generally have to rely on detailed information from the texts of the early missionaries. The same persons that tried to convert the people to another religion became paradoxically the main resources for conserving their memory. For my study, I can only with difficulty read their original texts written in ancient versions of various Scandinavian languages. Håkan Rydving composed an bibliography regarding the history of Sámi religion (Rydving 1993). He analysed in detail the sources concerning the Lule Sámi pre-Christian religion at time of the religious changes in the seventeenth and eighteenth centuries (1993: 27–34). In an other book, he

---

24 Some of the most known established scholars of the past three decades who researched Sámi religiosity and its links to nature and landscape are Louise Bäckman, Phebe Fjellström, Åke Hultkranz, Juha Pentikäinen, Håkan Rydving, Hans Mebius, Elina Helander Renvall, Siv Ellen Kraft, Audhild Schanche, Marit Myrvoll, Jelena Porsanger, Rauna Kuokkanen, Jorunn Jernsletten, Trude Fonneland, Rolf Christoffersson, Cato Christensen.

made the content of key ancient texts written by Danish-Norwegian missionaries easily available in a thematic synopsis that I used for this study (Rydving 1995). As to the places they describe, Rydving (1995: 27–42, 2010: 57ff) has composed overviews and drawn maps indicating from what precise Sámi areas people like the Danish-Norwegian priest Thomas von Westen and the Swedish missionaries gathered information. He also mentions which theological concerns influenced their missionary work and how this affected the content of their recordings. In some cases, however, it is only possible to venture a guess as to which Sámi area the specific information came from. Scholars like Holmberg-Harva, Bäckman, Mebius and others have recorded quotations and done equally extensive analyses of the ancient sources. Itkonen and Pentikäinen were useful for their records of oral local information and their references to ancient texts.

The accounts of the missionaries have limitations that are highly relevant to this research. Rydving describes them as follows:

> There were Sámi among the authors of these accounts, but most of the authors came from other cultures, had another religion, spoke other languages and were intent on replacing the indigenous religion with another belief. (…) There is nothing to indicate that their questions were relevant to the essentials of Sámi religion (2010: 58).

And also the Swedish scholar specializing in Sámi religion, Hans Mebius, drew similar conclusions from the ancient missionary texts:

> It was this mythological and ritual knowledge of the *noaidi* that above all interested Thomas von Westen and his colleagues. The beliefs of the common people about invisible beings other than those from the heavens or atmospheric, earthly and subterranean god-figures did obviously not raise the same amount of interest (Mebius 2007: 92).[25]

It can therefore not be surprising that the ancient missionary recordings did not often mention most of the superhuman agents discussed in this research. In addition, the issue of how to keep ecological balances with the local environments was not addressed 250 years ago. Probably those types of values

---

25 "Det var denna mytologiska och rituella kunskap hos nåjderna som framför allt intresserade Thomas von Westen och hans kollegor. Gemene mans föreställningar om andra osynliga väsen än de himmelska, atmosfäriska, jordiska och underjordiska gudagestalterna väckte uppenbarligen inte samme intresse" (Mebius 2007: 92).

and concerns were either so widespread that they were considered to be generally known or they were considered insignificant in times before the ecological crisis.

Contemporary Sources: First Half of the Twentieth Century

At the turn of the nineteenth to the twentieth century, scholars like Qvigstad systematically collected local oral stories and at the same time, the first Sámi began to produce writings themselves. Among them are the five authors besides the interviews I have referred to most frequently in my analysis. Jelena Porsanger has researched the types of the sources for the Sámi religious traditions of the Eastern Sámi and categorized texts in primary and secondary sources (Porsanger 2007: 82–90). Decisive criteria for her are if the oral narratives were recorded and transcribed in original languages, so that cultural contexts like irony or hidden meanings can be researched and that the sources are are properly contextualized. That means that we have to know the names of the persons who spoke to a researchers. Some of the stories of Qvigstad qualify as primary sources due to their thourough recordings. The text of Johan Turi is a very important primary source. T.I. Itkonen's book from 1946 (Porsanger 2007: 302–305) and Holmberg' s book from 1915 (Porsanger 2007: 308–309) are considered as secondary sources.

Johan Turi (1854–1936) was a reindeer-herding Sámi who migrated between the Karesuando area and the Norwegian-Swedish mountain areas. He had been working as a guide for rich foreigners who were very interested in Sámi culture, and describes how they often simply did not understand it. Therefore, Turi himself wanted to write about the essential aspects of Sámi life, as he knew it. This plan could be realized when he met the Danish artist Emilie Dermant-Hatt, as she made his notes and drawings ready for publication. Turi's texts are of fundamental importance for knowledge about Sámi culture and Sámi self-understanding. He makes many interesting observations about the relationships between Sámi and non-Sámi. His texts were recently re-edited in various language editions and are much read and discussed today.[26]

---

26 The magazine *Sámi diedalas áigečála* 2/2011 and 1/2012, published by the Sámi University College in Kautokeino, Norway, had a double issue on J. Turi with online abstracts in English: http://site.uit.no/aigecala/.

Knut Just Qvigstad (1854–1957) has provided the most important source for Sámi traditional stories in the Norwegian Sámi area, recorded at the end of the nineteenth century and published in the 1920s in four large volumes. Qvigstad was principal of the teachers' academy in Tromsø, linguistic expert in Finnish, Kvenish and Sámi, a teacher, a leader of education and cultural institutions, a politician and a folklore expert. He had engaged a local network of contact persons who thoroughly recorded the stories in the way they were told and written down in both Northern Sámi and Norwegian. Qvigstad's project certainly also had its biases in terms of the content and type of stories told. Porsanger considers texts that were recorded by persons who knew Sámi and who worte down the name of the source as primary souces (Porsanger 2007: 179), while others, that were not written down in their original Sámi languages or lacked other contextual informations, are cateforized as secondatory sources (Porsanger 2007: 318–319).

Paavo Ilmari Ravila (1902–1974) was a Finnish linguist and researcher who recorded the statements of Jouni Nuorgam – who was an injured young Sámi reindeer herder from the Inari area – in the now extinct Northern Inari Sámi language. His texts give proof that many traditional rituals and sacrifices were still in use at the time of the recordings, in the first decade of the nineteenhundreds.

T. I. Itkonen (1865–1925) was a Finnish historian and linguist. He was the son of a Finnish cleric who was placed in Inari and grew up there. In the course of a number of research trips there, he recorded stories from the area where he grew up from Sámi indivuals in their respective Sámi languages, many if which are transcribed and kept in archives (Porsanger 2007: 147–148, 150–151, 327). Itkonen's book from 1946 also incorporates the fieldwork of others and makes generalizations that are based on informations that are not contextualized (Porsanger 2007: 304, 337). Itkonen encountered many living traditions of species-related guardian-spirit stories but he only wrote a few lines about them, in total a single page. He focuses on outer and "exotic" expressions like bizarre spirits and rituals, and he says little about inner values and beliefs.

Uno Holmberg (1882–1949, after 1927 was his name Harva) was a Finnish protestant theologian and minister who decided to work as a scholar in the history of religion and an ethnographer. He studied exiting texts about Sámi, and only later, in the 1920ties did fieldwork in the Eastern Sámi area (Porsanger 2007: 183, 308–311, 337).

Personal Interviews

For my interviews I selected three key informants – Laila Spik (Jokkmokk), Sigvald Persen (Stabbursnes) and another person from Tana who chose to remain anonymous. In the course of the research, Solveig Tangeraas, also from Sigvald Persen's local community, joined in as an informant.[27] Various Sámi individuals also offered spontaneous information that was later included in my research.

The criteria for selection of the informants were the following: 1) they had to be born before ca. 1950 and have experienced childhood and adolescence in the traditional subsistence society that existed in many areas until the mid-1960s; 2) they had to be respected as bearers of tradition in their own local community; 3) they had to have some overview over Sámi culture so as to be sure that they could proffer information that was representative and reliable; 4) they had to be interested and able to talk to me about religious beliefs and rituals without this disturbing them or regretting it afterward, as many persons like to keep these things to themselves; 5) they had to be motivated, wishing to make a contribution to the spread of knowledge about the beliefs and practice of the Sámi; 6) they had to possess some long-term perspective in discussing Sámi issues and the development of projects to support local Sámi culture; 7) they had to personally agree to talk with me.

As to my relationship with them prior to the research, I have known Laila for ten years and Sigvald for five and had collaborated with them in the coordination of several projects. I have also visited Laila regularly at her summer dwelling in Saltoluokta, and she came to Bergen during the work on my present thesis.

Regarding anonymity, Laila, Sigvald and Solveig wished to provide information under their real names. Sigvald stated that it would feel like a "theft" if I did not mention that I had recorded statements from him. Solveig thought it just fine that readers knew what information came from her. The disadvantage of this kind of openness is that the informant may be more circumspect in divulging information with which they will be associated in the public realm. Any sensitive information can be hidden, and it is not easy

---

27 Their names are abbreviated in the text. SP = Sigvald Persen, ST = Solveig Tangeraas, LS = Laila Spik, MB = Mardoeke Boekraad.

to admit that something is sensitive and that one wishes to hide it. I think that this conscious self-censorship took place to some degree, but it did not make the information that I did receive any less interesting.

Laila Spik lives in Jokkmokk and Gällivare in Sweden; she was born around 1948, is married with one child, is trained as as a teacher, is a reindeer holder, and makes her living as a cultural worker and as a gastronomic expert in Sámi traditional cuisine. She is a member of the Swedish state church but has a great affinity to ancient pre-Christian practices. Her father was lule Sámi and her mother northern Sámi. Her father Jovva was very much aware of the loss of ancient traditions, wished to preserve as many of them as possible, and transmitted them to his daughter Laila (Bornstein 2002: ch. 20). She masteres both Sámi languages.

Spik appears regularly on television programs where she explains Sámi culture and has co-published a biographical book under the title *Den samiske vandringsrösten, -Jag är kunskapen* (Bornstein 2002). She is probably one of the most outspoken contemporary Sámi on issues concerning Sámi traditional religion and spirituality.

Sigvald Persen lives in Stabbursnes in Porsanger in Western Finnmark in Norway. He was born in 1948, is divorced and has two children. He is a Sea Sámi from the coastal area and grew up in a household where they kept sheep and made their living from fishing, small-scale hunting and handicrafts. His parents were Læstadians[28] and he is a member of the state church, but not an active churchgoer. Sigvald is an educated engineer and worked many years for the local municipality before deciding to co-found the Sea-Sámi competence center[29] in Indre Billefjord. He is also known as a local traditional healer who does not takes payment for his services. He has written several articles about local knowledge for joint projects with Tromsø University and contributed with his life experience to a PhD dissertation "Connecting and Correcting: A Case Study of Sámi Healers in Porsanger" (Miller 2007). I met him when working on a project on traditional values (see note 19).

---

28 A Christian charismatic movement founded by Lars Levi Læstadius (1800–1866) that had strong influence amongst many Sámi communities.

29 Mearrasámi diehtoguovddáš, Sjøsamisk kompetansesenter, in Indre Billefjord/ Billávuotna, Norway.

Solveig Tangeraas lives in Indre Billefjord. She is a retired teacher and active in the local Sámi cultural association. She was born around 1940, is married and has several children.

The informant from Tana wished to be anonymous. The older and younger members of that family discussed the issue of my research and considered it important that their family traditions be recorded and made available for scholarly debate. They wished to remain anonymous because the elderly members of the family did not want their traditions to be known by the local priest and their neighbors, as they feared that negative judgment would be passed on them.

How the Interviews Went

Because I did not have to devote any time in getting acquainted with the informants, it was sufficient to pay a visit of a few days at a time. I visited Sigvald three times for periods of one to three days (November 2012, February 2013, April 2013). I met with a local handicrafts club and their members during one of these visits, and I had a shared interview lasting for about four hours with Sigvald and Solveig during the last visit. I visited Laila Spik one week in August 2012 for my research and, because I knew her well, we were able to communicate over the telephone. We had about four longer telephone conversations of between half an hour and an hour about the research subjects during the whole research period after I had sent her e-mails with prepared questions. I sometimes made recordings of the interviews and sometimes I just took notes. The interviews that I have transcribed from the recordings give me, in re-reading the texts again, better and more detailed records of what has been said than the notes taken after the other interviews. In all cases I had prepared a set of questions and tried to be a good listener without interjecting too much or trying to direct the answers (Fangen 2004: 178). I was trying to be very careful not to ask too many follow-up questions, if that felt inappropriate.

As I already knew about a number of practices, it was possible to record relatively quickly a fair amount of information. On the other hand I noticed that the fact that I knew them already and had changed roles from a friend to a researcher also had negative consequences. It made it difficult to address other issues than those we had already spoken about.

I did not want to "dig" for more information when feeling that my respondents had said what they wanted to express, even though I remained curious as to more explications. The informants told me things they had been thinking about and had decided consciously that they wanted them to be known.

Chapter 3 – Sámi Backgrounds

In this chapter I will give some background information on the Sámi people, their languages and brief elements of their religious history. Then their ecological history and my understanding of "traditional Sámi culture" will be addressed. Last but not least I will discuss the way in which Sámi themselves describe their relationship to nature, what attitudes they have toward it, and how the Sámi worldview includes religious beliefs in reference to ecological sustainability. This background information serves as the preparation for introducing I. Paulson's categories of beliefs and rites in a spatial dimension, which will serve as an organizing principle for the following chapters.

3.1 On the Sámi people and Languages Today

The Sámi are a group of linguistically and culturally heterogeneous peoples. They are composed of about ten different language groups, several of which are extinct.[30] A person is considered as Sámi when at least one ancestor from at least three or four generations back in time spoke the Sámi language. These criteria are formalized; enrolling in these registers came into being in the 1980s and 1990s.[31] There are about 70,000 Sámi who live in four countries,[32] and it is estimated that about 34,000 of them speak Sámi. Around 90 percent of these Sámi speakers speak Northern Sámi and about two thousand speak

---

30 See the English pages of "Samiskt Informationscentrum", an official online Sámi information center financed by the Swedish Sámi parliament at www.eng.samer. se/ (read on 30.6.2015). Statistics Norway publishes regular reports in English entitled "Sámi Statistics."

31 The rules are slightly different in each country and concern an objective language-based criterium, as one of the great-grandparents has to have spoken Sámi; in Sweden persons married to Sámi can join. For details, see: Sametingets valgregelutvalg 30 September 2001.

32 Circa 2000 Eastern Sámi in Russia on the Kola Peninsula, 5000 to 6500 Eastern, Northern and Inari Sámi in Finland, 40,000 to 45,000 Northern, Lule, and Southern Sámi in Norway, and 17000 to 20 000 Northern, Lule, Pite and Ume Sámi in Sweden. Sámi form a minority in all places they live, with the exception of two municipalities in Norway and one in Finland: Kautokeino, Karasjok and Utsjoki.

Lule Sámi, the second largest Sámi language. Sámi are legally recognized as indigenous peoples in all coutries they live in.

Sámi people are economically and socially relatively well integrated into the modern states.[33] One cannot distinguish a Sámi house or person from a non-Sámi Norwegian, Swedish, Russian or Finnish one. The Sámi go to state schools, pay the same taxes and have the same civil rights, duties and professional education as all other citizens. However, with regard to their social situation, a recent study[34] in Norway shows that the most significant problem is that Sámi experience twice as much harassment as Norwegians and that Sámi women living outside of the Sámi areas have poorer health than those living inside the Sámi areas and that men have a higher suicide rate.

3.2 Change, Suppression and Diversity

Sámi culture has been recognizable through its archeological artifacts for at least 3000 years (Hansen & Olsen 2004: 31–41). The Sámi language is part of the Finno-Ugric language family and began developing as a separate language from a common proto-Finnish tongue circa 1500 BC (Hansen & Olsen 2004: 134, quoting Pekka Sammallahti). The self-designation of "Sámi" has been related to a reconstructed original word *šämä*, which signifies "land" (Hansen & Olsen 2004: 47).

By no means have the Sámi been a culturally isolated people. They had a semi-nomadic lifestyle and were continuously in contact with the surrounding agricultural societies and with the eastern part of Russia (Hansen & Olsen 2004: 32–33). None of the texts from the Middle Ages see them as impoverished or inferior (Hansen & Olsen 2004: 151). The colonialization of those areas which the Sámi inhabited and traditionally exploited had its beginnings in the thirteenth century (Hansen & Olsen 2004: ch. 3). The Sámi now became more strongly integrated into international trade networks. They provided fur and fish that they sold to traders from the town of Bergen and

---

33 For a recent critical report made on the human rights situation of Sámi by United Nations' Special Rapporteur on the rights of Indigenous Peoples, Prof. James Anaya, entitled "The situation of the Sámi people in the Sápmi region of Norway, Sweden and Finland (2011)" Doc nr. A/HRC/18/35/Add.2.

34 "Kunnskapsstatus likestilling blant Samer" Av Ketil Lenert Hansen, Universitet i Tromsø. September 2012.

the "birkarlere" on the Swedish-Finnish side (Hansen & Olsen 2004: chs. 3 and 4). The taxation systems that were imposed on the Sámi in particular in the period from the fifteenth to the seventeenth centuries placed a heavy burden on the Sámi communities. The Sámi were still considered a distinct and equal nation to others in the 1751 international treaty of Strömstad (also called the Lapp Codicil) which regulated migrating rights for reindeer herders across national borders (Hansen & Olsen 2004: 273–280). Afterward the states started imposing increasing amounts of regulations that affected the Sámi, for instance on trade. Farmers from the south could without Sámi consent appropriate the lands that they had been using for reindeer grazing. The reindeer-grazing lands thus became more restricted (Hansen & Olsen 2004: ch. 5). The closure of state borders due to separate nation-building had grave consequences for the migration routes of the reindeer herders. In the nineteenth century the Sámi were exposed to the discriminatory effects of social Darwinism; in Norway, to an official assimilation policy called Norwegianization, "Fornorskning," and in Sweden to the condescending policy of "A Lapp Must Remain a Lapp" (Lehtola 2004: 44–48). Many Sámi children in Norway were forced to attend boarding schools far from their home communities where they became alienated from their culture and their own relatives (Lehtola 2004: 62), others were only given restricted education in tent schools in Sweden. It was forbidden to use Sámi language at schools in Norway. In the 1960s the assimilation policies came to an end. After the large civil movement – linked to plans to build a huge hydroelectric dam close to Alta in Norway – there began a process of institutionalizing Sámi rights and cultures. This had important consequences on the cultural level. According to Lehtola a new flowering of the culture started, a kind of Sámi cultural renaissance took place (Lehtola 2004: 70, 76).

The *siida* was the basic social unit of the ancient Sámi society, at least in the Northern Sámi areas. In the course of history various types of *siida* were developed (Hansen & Olsen 2004). A *siida* consists of a group of individuals and families living together and covering an area in which the group undertook their seasonal migrations. Most *siida*'s stretched from the seacoast to the inlands. The *siida* did not have a hierarchical structure, even if it was usual that one particular respected person was the *siida*-leader. It had normally the full authority and exclusive usage rights over its local resources. The *siida* became increasingly weakened with the growing influence of state authorities and were totally dismissed in Finland with establishment of local state municipalities in the course of the nineteenth century (Lehtola 2004: 42). Many authors have described the ways in which locals divided the natural resources between them (Hansen & Olsen 2004: passim) and in an expert study for the Norwegian authorities Elina Helander-Renvall described the situation in the local areas (2001). Every lake, berry land and section of river was attributed to a person or family who had exclusive rights of use. This was the system in many places until the wave of modernization after World War II, and small pockets of it remain in in localities such as the village I lived in. Fewer and fewer people have the time to go fishing in inland lakes nowadays (oral information from locals, MB). Most people know in which lakes their family used to fish in the old days and which berry fields were theirs.

Religion is embedded in culture and transforms itself along with the historical development of societies. The ancient pre-Christian religion was based on oral and not written transmission and must therefore be reconstructed. We know that there were substantial differences between local religious expressions. For instance there are about six different designs and drawings of drums in the different Sámi regions. One some the sun is the central element, on others it is not (Christoffersen 2010). Also the names of the superhuman agents varied.

> There was never any uniform Sámi or Scandinavian religion, but important regional and individual variations, although the condition of the sources makes it tempting to generalize on weak grounds. (Rydving 2010: 25.)

Around the year 1000 the Norwegian kings became Christian. The first churches were built in the Sámi area in the eleventh and twelfth centuries. Several Sámi became committed Christians before and after the Reformation, which became the only officially allowed religion in Norway in 1537 by a decree of King Christian III. The union of the state and church was constantly strengthened. In 1593, the Lutheran Christian faith became the state religion in Sweden and in 1660, the state also appointed the clergy in the Norwegian/Danish kingdom. The Churches of Norway and Sweden became state churches which had over the centuries important roles in the administration of the states. In 1735, the confirmation Holy Communion became compulsory in Danmark/Norway. Other religious organizations were formally forbidden in the Norway until 1845, and in Sweden until 1851.

It is reported that Norwegians were afraid to immigrate to areas where Sámi lived because of their supposed magical skills (Hansen & Olsen 2004: 345). The sixteenth and seventeenth centuries was the period of witch trials. Proportionally fewer Sámi were executed than Norwegians. Sámi ceremonial drums were confiscated, sacred altars destroyed, wooden idols were burned. About 27 Sámi were executed because of witchcraft in the period 1593–1682. In Sweden the figures are much lower (Hansen & Olsen 2004: 324–327). In the Lule Sámi areas the pre-Christian religion went underground in the period from the 1670s to the 1740s (Rydving 1993). After the witch-hunt period, missionaries strengthened their efforts to Christianize the Sámi more intensively (Rydving 1993, 1995, 2010; see 2004 for an overview). Different groups of Sámi had different types of responses to the imposed religious change; some liked the new faith and became active supporters whereas others remained passive or neutral. A group of traditional activists continued in secret with ancient practices and condemned the new religion (Rydving 2004: 106).

In the mid-eighteenth century Sámi priest Lars-Levi Læstadius (1800–1866) led the lay religious revivalist movement that still has many adepts today (Minde 1998). There is a scholarly debate going on as to whether Læstadianism had so much success because it included elements of the ancient religion like healing, public ecstasy, visions and the like; in general the Læstadian movement resembles other charismatic movements of its time in Europe (Minde 1998, quoting Gjessing and Zorgdrager).

3.3 Traditional Sámi Culture

The term "traditional Sámi culture" has been discussed by several Sámi academics (Helander 1996, Guttorm 2011, and compare Bergström 2001). Polyani defined traditional experiential knowledge[35] and his ideas were transferred to the Sámi context by Sámi academics Maja Dunfjeld and Gunvor Guttorm (2011). Traditional knowledge is conceived as a custom

---

35 There are several Sámi University College projects on traditional knowledge, like "Ealát," "Birgen" and "Árbediehtu".

that is repeated for at least three generations (Polanyi referred to in Gut-torm 2011: 66).[36]

Traditional knowledge is linked originally to the traditional society where people relied on that type of knowledge to survive. This kind of traditional society structure, based on local communities that were to a large degree self-sufficient, remained predominant in many places in Northern Scandi-navia until about the mid-1960s (Kalstad 1996: 30, Aas e.a, 2010: 20 for a geographical description, Sara quoted in Guttorm 2011: 66). Within two decades after World War II the introduction of motorized transport such as the snow scooter, the building of year-around accessible asphalt roads to remote villages, and the general installment of electricity in houses became a fact in even the most remote Sámi areas (Aas ea. 2010: 20).

The skills, knowledge, attitudes, values and religious rituals related to the ancient life style is called "traditional knowledge" today. Much of it is not used any more or has already been forgotten. The context of this knowledge has completely changed; there exists an immense challenge to find new roles for this type of knowledge in modern society.

Traditional ecological knowledge is a concept that is used in the natural sciences (e.g. Fikret Berkes 1999/2012) for describing knowledge of the ecol-ogy or animal life of local tribal or indigenous peoples. It is based on the fact that indigenous peoples including Sámi were keen observers of nature and had a rich vocabulary related to it.[37] The recording of this type of knowl-edge has become the object of numerous local projects.[38] This thesis aims at documenting some of the religious aspects of that.

---

36 Traditional knowledge consists of a personal experience-based knowledge called "máhttu," such as observing a cloudberry field from year to year, and cannot be transmitted by the theoretical teaching of "diehtu" (knowledge) (Guttorm 2011: 68).

37 At the Sámi University College and cultural center, it is a regular type of project to collect ancient Sámi words from elderly people for Sámi terms referring to nature.

38 The Norwegian Institute for Cultural Heritage support (NIKU) recently concluded a project on recording local information concerning changes in fjord ecology at the Porsanger fjord known as "Fávvlis." The Finland-based "Snowchange" project links universities with local indigenous communities all over the Arctic and records signs of climate change. The Sámi University College project "EALAT" concerns traditional knowledge in reindeer herding.

3.4 *Birgejupmi*: Are Sámi Ecologically Sustainable?

The term "ecological sustainability" is linked to emergence of the environmental crisis and became part of the international agenda as a result of its use in the 1987 Brundtland report "Our Common Future." The question is whether this term can be used for the time before that crisis. The human need to use natural resources in a balanced way would not seem to be new – quite the opposite. Probably every culture had more or less effective ideologies and strategies for keeping intact the resources on which they lived, even if civilization can collapse due to ecological mismanagement.[39] Therefore it would make seeming sense that the term "ecological sustainability," even if new, should also be applied to that time before formal appearance of the term – just as the term "genes" can be used to talk about genes in a time before DNA was described.

The basic assumption of this thesis is that the traditional locally based Sámi subsistence culture, seen from the contemporary perspective, had sustainable patterns in various parts of the ecosystems. There might have been local natural resources that were used in such a way that they were not depleted in the long term, over many centuries, maybe even millennia. This does not rule out that some species came under pressure as a result of overhunting due to heavy taxation, like the beaver that might have disappeared from northern Norway.[40] The Great Auk (*Pinguinus impennis*) bones of most recent date found in Norway are from the Stone Age. About 150 years ago this bird species suffered worldwide extermination. It was an easy-to-hunt and tasty auk-like, flightless bird living on the coasts of the North Atlantic. To my disappointment it was rather difficult to find information on this subject in relation to the Sámi; studies do not relate traditional knowledge to the biological expertise of outsiders. Such studies would be very interesting for further analysis of the ecological history of the Sámi areas but, as long they have not been made, it is rather difficult to assert that "the Sámi" had an overall 100 percent or even 80 percent ecologically sustainable pre-modern

---

39 See Diamond Jared, 2005, *Collapse, How Societies Choose to Fail of Succeed*, Viking Press, New York.

40 Information acquired during my work in Sirma/Finnmark in 2006. Sámi place-names in the Tana area refer to beaver even if they were extinct for centuries. A number of beavers have recently been reintroduced into Northern Norway.

culture. To my knowledge the ancient Sámi subsistence economies' impact on ecological balances had not yet been critically analyzed. The general assumption is that the Sámi did not damage local ecosystems over long periods of time in which they used the resources almost entirely themselves.

Traditionally scholars have described Sámi religion as well adapted to the environment and close to nature, even if not as sustainable or pointed toward keeping balances. Åke Hultkrantz, in his article "Religion and Environment among the Saami: An Ecological Study" (1994) does not make specific references to sustainability: "Whenever practiced by hunters, fishermen or pastoral nomads, Saami religion remained close to nature in its expression and well adapted to environmental demands" (Hultkrantz 1994: 367). Hultkranz sees the Sámi as part of a circumpolar hunting culture that has "animal ceremonialism" as an important characteristic: "Catching, killing and burial of game played a mayor role in everyday religion" (1994: 357). Also for Pentikäinen the central role of animals and the beliefs, rituals and rules related to them was a distinctive feature of Sámi religion (Pentikäinen 1997: 77–81, 323). Even rather critical voices agree that indigenous peoples and also Sámi have some kind of close relationship to their landscapes and nature: "Closeness to animals, nature and the divine are possibly characteristic for indigenous religions in general,"[41] states Siv Ellen Kraft (Kraft 2004: 244).

Scholars who write from a Sámi perspective and elaborate upon the Sámi worldview argue that the most important characteristic of that view is that everything in the universe has equal rights, is related and interconnected in a form of reciprocity, and has to keep balance in order to function well (Jernsletten 2004: 55–56, Kuokkanen 2000, Helander Renvall 2010). Jelena Porsanger mentions the concept of a close mutual relationship between Sámi and "everything in creation," of an "inseparable unification of people and nature" (Porsanger 2012: 39). In her view this close relationship has traditionally been reciprocal and can be considered as the very basis of the indigenous Sámi religion (Porsanger 2012: 37, 39.)

In Sámi language the traditional view of the relationship to the natural environment has been described by the term *birgejupmi*, translated as "maintenance of life" by J. Porsanger (Porsanger 2012: 38). *Birgejupmi* has

---

41 "Nærhet til dyr, naturen og det guddommelige er muligens kjennetegnende for urfolksreligionene generelt" (Kraft 2004: 244).

a number of translations that reflect its various aspects: "survival capacity" by John B. Hendriksen (2011) and "having enough to make a living" by Helander (1999: 20). *Birgejupmi* implies a broad spectrum of elements such as social aspects and a value system according to which none took more from nature than they needed to survive. *Birgejupmi* presupposes a view that everything in the world is interrelated and connected to the logic of sustainability.

Traditionally the aim of the Sámi people has not been to exploit natural resources in one spot an then to and move on to an other area, but rather to use local ressources in the most effective and rational manner. Survival in the North depending on a renewal of the riches of nature. Individuals and communities traditionally need to maintain balance with the limited number of local ecosystems they had acces to in order to make their living and ensure their well-being. This presupposes that people think about the world and themselves in a holistic and reciprocal way. *Birgejupmi* describes a holistic Sámi understanding of well-being and survival and the interdependence of everything in the world (Porsanger 2012: 39, 42).

This paraphrase shows that, from her Sámi perspective, Porsanger is consciously referring to the modern term sustainability and that this way of life has existed in a variety of economic structures. She apparently considers this term appropriate for addressing ancient cultural patterns; she is adhering to a holistic model of thought. Gods and animals, humans and all types of powers are part of a cooperative system. When one of the elements is missing then the relationship with the ecosystems is incomplete and dysfunctional. Superhuman agency is one of the elements that integral to the whole. The quote of Sigvald Persen also illustrates this very well:

> "One was dependent on a nature that entailed knowledge from the old times. Knowledge which was embedded in religious ritual elements that had disappeared. People had a religion on the basis of the old ways and that was taken away. 'We have liberated ourselves from nature,' they say. Religion is tied to the use of resources. Spirituality intervenes in material conditions – you have that as long as you depend on it, otherwise you cannot have it any more. It becomes artificial – just an experience."[42] (SP Oct. 2012.)

---

42 "Man var avhengig av naturen, det var kunnskap fra eldre tid. Kunnskap som ble innbunnet i religiøse rituelle elementer som ble borte. Man hadde et forhold som grunnlaget for det gamle og det ble tatt bort. 'Vi har frigjort oss fra naturen' sier

Sigvald explained that the ancient sustainable lifestyle was for him based on practical necessities and had no general supra-regional conservation ideology. "People in the old days hunted every single seal in the fjord they could. They knew that new seals always came" (Oct. 2013). According to him, the ancient lifestyle disappeared because of two factors: the changes in society, in that one could buy food from a shop, and the introduction of regulations that ended and forbid the traditional local ecological management practices. For instance in 1978 Sigvald himself lost the right to fish salmon from the local river with nets (Miller 2007: 199–205). Laila Spik is of the same opinion as Sigvald. Also for her, the Sámi lived in a sustainable way before change in the social model. She adds one factor to the two that he mentioned, namely the embarassment that some Sámi feel regarding their own traditional value system.

> "Not all Sámi are keeping the rules. Not everyone wishes to live like that. Some feel that it is inferior to be like that. They wish to be 'something better.' Today's people have mostly abandoned the knowledge. The unwritten rules. We live in a time of decadence."[42] (LS August 2012.)

Laila Spik is indirectly blaming the Sámi for being ashamed of themselves while at the same time indicating that she hopes that times might change. Sámi academic Rauna Kuokkanen also confirms that many Sámi are ashamed of their traditional values. A great deal of Sámi spiritual knowledge has been lost or destroyed by colonization and forced Christianization over several generations. Only remnants of this knowledge remain today, and many Sámi now see traditional Sámi spirituality, linked to living in a respectful relationship with the land, as insignificant and shameful.[43]

---

man. Religion er ja knyttet til bruk av ressurser. Åndelighet ingriper i materielle forhold. Så du har den så lenge du er avhengig av den. Ellers kan du ikke ha den lengre, det blir kunstig åndelighet, bare et opplevelse" (SP Oct 2012).

"Ikke alle samer holder seg til reglene. Ikke alle vil leve slik. De vil være 'fint' og ikke være samer. Dagens menneske har forlatt kunnskapene-'de uskrevne reglene.' Vi lever i en tid av forfall" (LS Aug. 2012).

43 Rauna Kuokkanen in an online published text, May 5, 2010: "Water Prospecting Threatens Sami Sacred Site." http://www.culturalsurvival.org/publications/cultural-survival-quarterly/finland/water-prospecting-threatenssami-sacred-site downloaded on 28 May 2013.

As to the traditional society, Laila Spik described in an interview her vison of the "round life" that she lived in the old days. For her things felt safe and much better than today. The tents and earth huts they lived in back then were round. Life became unsafe when the family started living in square houses (SP August 2012). At the end of our last interview, Solveig Tangeraas, who lives 1000 kilometers from Laila and is unacquainted with her, spontaneously used the same word "round" to describe the traditional life. She talked about the "round circle" of their harmonious life in former times (ST May 2013).

Jelena Porsanger proposes a holistic and relational model of thought. Gods and animals, humans and all types of powers are part of a cooperative system. When one of the elements is missing, the relationship with the ecosystems is incomplete and dysfunctional. Superhuman agency is one of the elements that is part of the whole. This concept of religion as inseparable from daily life and all other aspects of culture and society corresponds to criticisms leveled by people such as Talal Asad (see ch. 1). In modern Europe, secularism is the rule. And that might be difficult to combine with this certain concept of religion. At the same time, the difference between religion and cultural values and ideals, e.g. between superhuman agents and "powers," is smaller than ever before. Religious behavior becomes "culturalized" and often dissociated from centralized churches that have their own agendas. Herein might lie a cultural difference between indigenous and non-indigenous worldviews that deserves further research.

The Value-System behind *Birgejupmi*

The relations in this network of the ecosystem are based on ethics entailing the key notions of respect and reciprocity, an awareness that everyone is interdependent and has a duty to help one another as well as equality between the parties: "In principle creatures do have equal rights and can claim their share of that which is available at any point in time or which is accessible and necessary for their existence"[44] (Magga et al 2001: 3).

---

44 "I utgangspunktet er alle skapninger likeberettigete, og har krav på sin andel av det som til enhver tid tilbys eller er tilgjengelig og nødvendig for deres eksistens" (Magga, Oskal & Sara 2001: 3).

Many Sámi refer to a set of traditional values regarding how to treat nature and each other respectfully. I have encountered this mentioned set of values everywhere I go.[45] It appears to be a coherent and idealistic system of basic values vis-à-vis humans and nature which is taught to children from the youngest age. Magga stated that Sámi values with regard to nature are well documented (Magga 2011). Some of its concrete elements are that nothing – animals, plants or even stones – was to be disturbed without important and serious reason. One should never touch a wild animal, destroy or even blow over a birds' nest, make noise when outdoors, especially close to water, so as not to scare the fish away. Children were not allowed to break twigs from trees without reason or turn over stones for fun because it could disturb the insects underneath; neither were they allowed to walk off the path so as not to tread on vegetation. In short, children were taught to treat animals and plants in the same careful manner as fellow human beings. There also existed many rules related to hunting, probably so as to make sure that animal populations would remain in balance. The transgression of these rules can result in sanctioning a superhuman agency in the form of various degrees of bad luck. These rules have an obvious significance in a context of sustainability. They aim at the optimal well being of all living creatures and confirm the idea that everything around us is alive and supports us if one behaves only well. I will return to these rules in the following chapters. (Information from the aforementioned project and Magga 2011, and information LS, SP and ST.)

3.5 Structuring Beliefs Related to Ecological Sustainability

For my analysis of the structure of the religious beliefs and behaviors, I have chosen a spatial division that goes from the individual to the global. It is inspired by the typology of wild animal spirits proposed by the Estonian-Swedish scholar of the science of religion Ivar Paulson (1922–1966)[46] and

---

45 Sámi Traditional Knowledge about the Use of Nature, Sámi árbevirolaš čehppodat luonddugeavaheamis, 2008, was a project coordinated by me and directed by Niiilas A. Somby in 2008 and financed amongst other by the Sámi parliaments in Norway, Finland and Sweden, and the Nordic Council. It resulted in a low-budget documentary film with compilations of interviews of fourteen well-known Sámi traditional knowledge holders from four countries.

46 Ivar Paulson was an Estonian poet and ethnologist who worked in Sweden and had a broad knowledge of the Inuit, Finno-Ugric and Siberian cultures among

which serves as the basis of my research. The typology he gives of wild animal-related spirits in his publication *Wildgeister im Volksglauben der Lappen* (1961) goes as follows:

> 1. The soul that protects each individual animal; 2. The species-related spirits of each animal type[47]; 3. Owners and gods that stem from the animal world itself like *Leibolmai*; 4. Special hunting gods and godesses like *Juksakka*.
> 5. General and local nature spirits like spirits and gods of the forest and the water that are considered owners of the wild animals; 6. A special god in the range of "high gods" – the *corven radien*, "Horn Ruler" (Paulson 1961: 148).[48]

Paulson distinguishes individual and species spirits from *háldi*, the water or forest spirits, and draws a clear distinction between the species-protection spirits and the local-owner type of spirit, which he calls nature spirits. They have a more ownership-related role instead of a protective role. I have en-larged Paulson's categories to larger ones that also encompass superhuman agencies which are not based on animals. In my research, Paulson's categori-zation of animal-related spirits is extended to all things that are considered to have personhood in Sámi traditional religions, like trees and stones. Level 5 is extended to all forms of superhuman agency concerning local landscapes such as lakes, fjords or reindeer-grazing lands and other places watched over by underground spirits. The sixth level becomes the global level where one finds the gods, the nature as a sacred concept, and the pantheon of gods of the ancient Sámi religion. This typology has inspired the organization of the chapters on it. First I discuss level 1, the relations with the individual entities. In chapter 5, I address Paulsons type number 2, the species-related agencies

---

others. Paulson is most known for having elaborated upon the differences be-tween the body-related and free souls in the Sámi and other traditional cultures. According to the orbitary written by A. Hultkrantz (1966), his work "opens up the investigation of religions to ecological studies".

47 "It [category of species-related spirits, MB] corresponds entirely to the concep-tion of the species-related animal-protection spirit which has developed from the animal world itself" (My translation of Paulson 1961: 147).

48 1. Seele bzw Schutzseele des einzelnen Tieres; 2. Artgeister der einzelnen Tiergat-tungen; 3. Die aus der Tierwelt selbst hervorgewachsenen allgemeinen Tiereigner oder Gottheiten der Tiere und der Jagd wie, zB Leibolmai; 4. Die besondern Jagdgottheiten zB Juksakka; 5. Allgemeine und lokale Naturwesen-geister und Gottheiter des Waldes, bzw der Gewässer, als Eigner der wilden Tiere; 6. Eine spezielle Wildgottheit ist der "Horn Herrscher" (Paulson 1961: 148).

such as the ancestor animal, the species-related protection spirit called máddo and sacred animal species with the bear as an example. I have included the hunting god *Leibolmai* in the overall pantheon in chapter 7.3, which corresponds to Paulson's category 6. Spirits that stem directly from animals can be found in categories both 1 and 2. The general nature spirits figure in chapter 6. They are the underground people, the sacred shrines called háldi or sieidi and the personified landscape.

And figuring at the highest level is also the superhuman agency of "nature" taken as a whole.

There are a few interesting superhuman agencies and rituals that could not be treated in this study. One is the rituals related to the deposit of bones; another is other of the various species of sacred animal such as the magical bird called the "noaideloddi."[49] At each level I will analyze the functioning of the superhuman agency in terms of its significance for ecological sustainability.

---

49 *Noaide* was the religious expert or virtuoso of the ancient Sámi religion. The term is comprehensively described in Mebius 2007; and for the various terms for the *noaide*, see Rydving (2010: 73–92).

Chapter 4 – Superhuman Agency at the Individual Level

4.1 Animal Shape-Shifting

Stories about humans that transfigure into animals are frequent in traditional Sámi storytelling material (Kulonen 2005: 212–13, Tillhagen 1969, Qvigstad 1927 story no. 141, 143, Pentikäinen 1997: 88–91). Shape-shifting or theriantropic skills are said to be often, though not generally, the domain of religious experts. Persons can transform themselves into an animal out of free will and have the possibility of becoming human again. The chosen animals are normally wolves or bears, frogs or fish, and sometimes also mice or little birds. The aim can be to help someone else, to overcome an evil enemy in competition with another *noaidi*, or no reason must be given. Johan Turi took down a story of how subterraneans, in this case called "ulddat," transform a murderous group of Russian robbers into murderous wolves – against their will and without any possibility of returning to human shape (Turi 2011: 110). There are some descriptions of rather simple rituals from the Skolt-Sámi area with which everyone, even children, was said to be transformed into an animal and back again: circling three times around or under a pine tree that was bent to a curve, or doing a forward roll over a tree stump (Kulonen 2005: 213, Itkonen 1946: 121, Qvigstad 1927 I story no. 141, 143).

Sometimes it is told that a hunter or fisherman can encounter human objects like a belt, knife, money or shoelace under the skin of a hunted animal; these animals are regarded as former humans who became "bewitched" animals. They are dangerous and should not be hunted or eaten (Itkonen 1946: 120–121, Pentikäinen 1997: 85–86, Kulonen 2005: 13). In my interviews I did not focus on recording contemporary stories about shape-shifting because these may have been part of intimate personal realms or private mystical experiences and did not have ecological sustainability as their main theme.

Therianthropy enhances the keen observation of nature. It leads people to be constantly attentive to potentially strange behavior and other irregular aspects of wild animals since they could be transformed humans and thus bring bad luck with them.

Wild animals can have skills felt as desirable to humans. Animals can serve as ideal role models and teachers. Who would not like to imagine being as strong as a bear, to howl and run with the wolves or soar like an eagle? A temporary change of identity can also be seen as a psychological way of dealing with personal tensions, as a way of escaping the confines of one's physical body as well as the worries and stresses of daily life. Could it be compared – to be slightly provocative and without seeking to trivialize the mystical personal experience of shape-shifting – to why people today take vacations or go to the cinema?

Therianthropy shows how permeable and relative the boundary between humans and animals can be. The belief in therianthropy attenuates or even eliminates the idea of animals being generally "dangerous" or "other" and installs the concept of hybrid human/animal identities. Theriantropy implies identification and emotional attachment and in some cases the idealization of wild animals. Insofar it can become a powerful motivating factor for supporting the well-being of wild animals, like not to disturb individual animals and to respect and even protect those parts of the ecosystem that they depend on.

4.2 Non-Human Personhood[53]

For this study it was most appropriate to choose the type of belief system that has been described with the term "non-human personhood" (see ch. 1). It is often connected to animism (see earlier the theoretical chapter for a debate on terminologies). The term "personhood" avoids the discussion of the nature, absence or presence of a soul in Sámi culture. Animism was the notion of older Lapplogist scholars who were influenced by the evolutionistic views considered to be characteristic of Sámi religion, and therefore Pentikäinen prefers not to use it (Pentikäinen 1997: 323). It is mentioned as characterizing Sámi religion by a number of Sámi scholars (Bäckman 1975: 137, Schanche 1995: 43, Mulk 2000: 2 69, Jernsletten 2004: 54–55, Helander 2010: 45ff). The ancient missionary texts do not attest to the existence of this type of belief system (Mebius 2007: 25). It has been mostly promoted by contemporary scholars with a Sámi perspective. The concept of non-human personhood implies that every living being and also non-living objects like stones or drums[50]

---

50 "Ceremonitrummorna uppfattades som levande. Enlit Kildal kude nåjden kommunicera direkt med trumman.(…) Følge av konsekrationens ritual av trummer

and overarching units of the environment like landscapes or nature take an active subject-role, which means that they have agency. They have a superhuman personality with comparable qualities to humans, like conscious thinking, speaking, emotions and deliberated actions. They are also seen as having equal value to them. This has many consequences for people's relationship with the ecosystem (Helander 2010: 50). The information from my informants can be interpreted in that way. The two key informants consider the communication with non-human persons to be essential and indispensable for human survival in the local ecosystems, as we can see from the examples with the seabirds in this chapter and the fish *sieidi* in chapter 6.

The communication with non-human persons can take three basic forms: (a) animals and trees can be felt to be talking in regular human language, (b) in the form of symbolic information or (c) in giving messages through their behavior according to the system of animals' omens, called "diida." Johan Turi writes that all animals could speak in the old days and that they will speak again to accuse humans of all wrongs they have done on Judgment Day (Turi 1910).[51] Magga and others state that there are forms of spiritual

---

var 'at trumman ansågs ha blivit levande." [The ceremonial drum was considered to be alive. According to Kildal, the noaide could communicate directly with the drum. As a result of the consecration, it became alive.] (Christoffersen, 2010: 123, 124.)

51 "Ja boares áiggis leat hupman visot eallit ja muorat ja geaďđgit ja visot mii gávdo eatnama alde, ja nu galget hupmat maŋimus duomu áiggi nai.(...) Ja maŋimus beaivvi lea beana vuosttaš alaguoddi. Ja de maŋŋil ieža luonddogáhppálagat, mat leat olbmo hálddahusa vuolde- (...) Dan gal galgašii muitit juohkehaš, ahte ii leat ila garas su vuložiiddásis – leat go olbmot dahje luonddogáhppálagat." (Turi 1910/2010: 114) [And in the olden times all animals and trees and rocks and everything found on earth was able to talk. And they will all be able to talk again at the Last Judgment. And on the Last Day the dog will be the first witness for the prosecution. And after the dog all other animals of nature, which came under the man's control: those that had to work too hard or had been given too heavy burdens and who were beaten as well. Alas, the poor animals that do not have mouths with which to say that they can't pull any more! And then even people manage to hear their sorrowful voice, sometimes like a sigh. And it is so sorrowful a sound that it cuts right to the marrow of one's bones unless a person is of too harsh a nature.] (Turi 1910/2012: 123.)

communication between humans and animals.[52] Some Sámi I spoke to during my visits to the Sámi areas said that they and their families had never stopped talking to animals, while others confirmed that that is something only from the past. My informants considered communication with animals as autonomous and thinking subjects to be a natural part of their life and was regarded as a spiritual but not a sacred activity.

The relationship's essence is described as reciprocity implying mutual support and duties based on contract-like agreements. Humans have to ensure that everything around them, like animals and plants, will thrive and that the animals and all nature supports humans in return (Helander 2010: 50).

For instance animals and plants help humans to find medicine in the nature, and humans help seabirds to make their nesting areas safe from predators.

> You have mental contact with animals. One understands them and sometimes one has to interpret their replies. And thank them. We receive much from animals and plants. They heal us and give us good advice. How do we return this to them? Everything has a soul. Plants, landscapes, fish have a fish god that guarded the fish stock, everything. If I say that we speak with animals and plants, people get very confused. They do not understand that. We have survived in that way over thousands of years. How can we find medicine if we do not get that knowledge from the nature spirits? Knowledge and spirituality are connected and cannot be separated.[53] (LS Aug. 2012.)

Sigvald Persen stated that one cannot really take care of the sea bird population if one cannot communicate intuitively with animals. He explained this

---

52 "I følge den tradisjonelle forestillingsverden har naturen, som mennesket er totalt avhengig av, bade en åndelig og et materielt aspekt. Således må det være tilstede en tankemessig og verbal kommunikasjon i kontakten med naturen og dens ulike vesener, samtidig som mennesker gjennom praktiske handlinger påvirker naturen og selv blir påvirket av den." [According to the traditional world view, nature, on which humans are entirely dependent, has both a spiritual and material aspect. Therefore communication through thoughts and words has to exist in contact with nature and the different beings that inhabit it, at the same time as humans influence the nature with their practical handlings and are influenced by it.] (SP 2012.)

53 Du har mentalt kontakt med dyrene. Man forstår de og av og til må man tolke deres svarene. Og takker de. Vi får så mye av planter og dyr. De helbreder oss og gir råd. Hva gjør vi egentlig tilbake? Alt er besjelet. Planter, landskap, fisk har en fiskegud, den passer på fiskebestand, alt. Hvis jeg sier at vi snakker med dyr og vekst, blir folk helt forvirret. De forstår det ikke. Sånt har vi overlevd i årtusende. Hvordan finner vi medisin hvis vi ikke får fortalt det av naturånder? Kunnskap og åndelighet henger sammen og kan ikke adskilles. (LS August 2012.)

64

by telling a story about seabirds. Animals and humans cooperate by creating the best mutual benefit through contact with nature and its various entities, as humans simultaneously influence nature via practical acts just as nature influences them. (Magga, Oskal & Sara 2001: 5.) Predators can create great havoc and decimate seabird populations by robbing eggs and the juvenile bird before they can fly. The Sámi used to kill all predators, including eagles that came to those islands on the fjord where seabird colonies had their nests. Local Sámi were heavily dependent for food on the seabird eggs and ate some types of seabird meat as well. The seabirds, according to Sigvald, for their part purposely chose islands that were close to human settlements because they knew the humans would protect them. It was even normal – stated Sigvald – that the seabirds would have spiritual contact with the humans to tell them that a dangerous predator like a fox had swum to the island. The aim was that humans would come to shoot the fox and protect the bird's nest and youngsters. That system came to a forced ending when the national state authorities imposed legislation that prohibited the shooting of predators. A fact upon which all my key informants agree is that since then nature protection – e.g. in the case of seabirds but also for many other species – is totally ineffective because this type of traditional ecological knowledge has not been taken into account. Since the interdiction on hunting predators there are too many eagles and foxes; the nests of sea birds, including the almost extinct ones, are being plundered without respite.

Trees and Plants[54]

There are at least three sources from the turn of the nineteenth to the twentieth century from Northern, Skolt and Lule Sámi areas that mention individual tree spirits which require chopping and permisson rituals whose violation can lead to sanctions – and these sources are Itkonen, Qvigstad and Demant-Hetta. Some of the rituals they mentioned are found in use almost unchanged today (Johnsen 2005, Kalstad 1997: 24, oral information).

---

54 Originally I also planned to discuss in this paragraph the superhuman agency of stones but lacked time and space for that. This poem from a novel of Kirste Paltto, one of the best known contemporary Sámi writers shows amongst others the agency of a stone. The novel is worth reading and illustrates the Sámi religious worldview well. (Paltto, The White Stone, 1980/reedited in 2012.)

The reindeer-herding Sámi from Inari are of the opinion that every growing tree has a spirit (*muorra vuoiŋa*) that must be awakened before one cuts down the tree by striking three times with the steel of the ax against the stem. If one wishes to be precise one should also strike the places where the tree will be cut. Otherwise the fire can start to spark or the woodcutter suddenly die. This in the same way as when a Skolt Sámi goes to the forest to gather wood, before felling the tree, he 'knocks it out' by striking the shaft of the axe against the tree three times. If he forgets that then the fire in the stove will crack and whistle" (Itkonen 1946: 70–71).[55]

The *muorra-vuoiŋa* is mentioned once more in his text: one has to cut off the lowest branch of a tree before felling it so that the tree-spirit does not remain in the tree. If one does not do that, the tree fellers can fall ill or even die. It brought great misfortune to bring that lowest twig with the tree-spirits into the house. Also when taking a tree stem for making a baby cradle, the half stem must be buried if one is to be entirely certain that the tree spirit has left the wood of the cradle; otherwise the forest spirit could take possession of the child (Itkonen 1946: 262).

Every single tree that is felled must be used, as no resource should be wasted. In addition to attribution of personhood, this account conveys the moral that one never should take more than needed. Trees actively participate in Judgment Day according to an oral story recorded by Qvigstad.

One ought not cut trees and let them rot in the forest because otherwise they will raise a complaint on Judgment Day against the human that did this (Qvigstad 1920: 171).[56] Tree spirits were obviously very important and had to be treated with caution. The sanctions for transgression of these rules included the most severe punishments of all, namely death penalty or the theft of innocent babies, and condemnation on Judgment Day. It is therefore not surprising that some of these rituals have survived in certain places to the present day. In the oral

---

55 "Die Rentierlappen von Inari meinen, jeder wachsende Baum habe einen Geist (muorra vuoiŋa) den man vor dem Fällen erweckt, indem man dreimal mit dem Nacken er Axt gegen den Baum schlägt. Will man genau sein, auch auf den Stellen, woran den der Baum abgeschnitten wird; sonst gibt er beim Verbrennen Feuergarben, und der Holzfäller erleidet einen plötzlichen Tod. (…) Desgleichen schlägt der Koltalappe, wenn er in den Wald geht, um Holz zu holen, vor dem Fällen einmal mit dem Nacken der Axt gegen den Baum, 'erschlägt ihn' wenn er es unterlässt, zischt und kracht das Feuer im Herd" (Itkonen 1946: 262).

56 "Man darf keine Bäume fällen und verfaulen lassen in Wald, sonst erheben diese beim jüngsten Gericht Klage gegen den betreffenden Menschen." (Qvigstad 1920: 171).

traditions Tore Johnsen reports that in his fieldwork one person told him that "one has to beat the tree so it becomes unconscious" before felling it (Johnsen 2005: 24). This is comparable to the slaughter of reindeer whereby the reindeer first is rendered unconscious before it dies.

A friendlier and less grim piece of information about contact between humans and trees is the following observation. According to Emilie Demant Hatt in a publication from 1928: "the Lapp girls, when returning from the heights to the forest districts in the autumn, hurried to embrace and greet the trees" (quoted in Hultkrantz 1994: 361). Here it seems that the girls behave toward trees as they would toward their personal friends. There is an emotional attachment to the trees. It may be significant that it is a woman who wrote down this girlhood tradition. Women were traditionally not too involved in hunting and fishing (Mebius 2007: 95, oral information LS) but rather in harvesting trees and plants.

I have encountered one ancient type of ritual asking for permission to harvest trees and plants. This information was received from only one informant, Laila Spik. In her family tradition all harvesting of trees or removal of individual trees must be proceeded by a permission ritual. This consists of three phases: first one intuitively tunes into the tree or plants. Secondly one asks with or without words inward permission to harvest them. The last phase is that one receives a reply. The reply can be yes or no and can be felt in the form of a physical attraction or repulsion to the tree or plant or even heard as a voice within.

That advice should be followed. The reason behind a "no" can be that the plants need to be there for a certain requirement of the local ecosystem, stated Laila, or because their plant population does not tolerate any extractions at that moment (LS August 2012, May 2013).

Sigvald Persen did not confirm the use of this type of explicit permission ritual when chopping trees. Laila Spik and Sigvald Persen both explained to me that it is an important ecological value that one should not be able to see any traces of human intervention in nature, for example traces of harvesting plants or trees in a forest. On the contrary, humans should help to make the species better.[57] To illustrate this, Sigvald showed me a birch-tree forest close

---

57 "Cultural Heritage in Northern Scandinavian Old Forests" in Norwegian "Kulturarvet I Nordskandinaviska Gammelskogar" (KING) project took place in

to his house which looked entirely natural even though he and his family had gathered firewood there for several decades or more.

> It should look like a natural forest. One should not see that I take lots of wood there. I mostly take old trees, so that the younger ones can grow better (SP March 2013).

Contracts of Reciprocity

The relationship between humans and animals is characterized by a value system that considers reciprocity the norm. This reciprocity implies binding mutual obligations. A number of orally transmitted mythological narratives attest to the conceptualization of human-animal relations and the form that this type of customary agreement and cooperation is based on. Sámi scholars refer to these as a basis for the Sámi ethical system (Magga, Oskal & Sara 2001: 2, 3). If the rules are not respected, since animals cannot directly defend or speak for themselves, the sanctions are being applied via superhuman intervention.

For instance dogs are an animal species that have concluded a contract with humans for mutual benefit (Magga, Oskal & Sara 2001: 2). Dogs were once wild animals but then one dog promised to work for man if he fed him decently and killed him respectfully when he grew old. So as to regulate the respectful keeping of reindeer there is a story of the two women Áhceseatni and Njáveseatni, according to which the reindeer stays with the kind woman who takes gentle care of it while leaving the other woman who then dies of hunger (Qvigstad II 1928: 327). The human relationship with the spider is described in a story about the spider helping a human to survive by weaving

---

2011–2013 and was a transfrontier project in which there is cooperation between an academic institution, Västerbotten museum and Árran, a local Sámi cultural center. This project was able to show that the ancient Sámi in this Lule-Sámi region harvested fir-tree bark in a way that distinguished them from the surrounding Norwegian villages. In the past, tree bark was an important source for food. Sámi did not cut down whole trees but had a special technique for taking bark from living trees without killing them. The fir trees that Sámi had been using for food in the nineteenth century were still alive over 300 years later. See book "Kulturarv I Gammelskog" (Skogsstyrelsen 2013) and in English: Rautio, A-M., Josefsson, Östlund L., 2014. Sami Mobility Patterns and Resource Utilization: Harvesting Inner-Bark in northern Sweden. Human Ecology, 42 (1): 137–147.

a web to hide the Sámi from passing murderers. The spider is rewarded with eternal protection by all humans (Qvigstad I 1926: 151). In these situations, man and animals are considered to be equal partners and the humans are held responsible for treating the animal respectfully.

Is this apparently harmonious relationship of all beings doing all they can to share their gifts, help each other and behave nicely and politely toward one another a romantic interpretation? There is another source that is harsher and contradicts an overly idyllic picture of these formal contractual relations, namely J. Nuorgam as transcribed by Ravila. The Inari-Sámi word for "war" is here used for the rituals against the cold, the drought and the death of dogs (Ravila 1934: 33–35). He also describes a ritual from the Inari reindeer-herding Sámi to be held in October by reindeer herders to trace lost reindeer; it designates predators to reindeer as the "enemy."[58] The herders hope to recover lost animals alive and not devoured by predators. The ritual involves three men: one who pours blood on a stone, one who sacrifices and one who is "defender of the predators" and defends the spirits of the forests and the robbing predators. The "defender of the predators" is a naked man dressed only in a belt with a knife in it. His task is to try to sneak toward the stone and the fireplace where a reindeer liver is placed on a stick and then manage to throw his knife on it. The ritual must be repeated until the "defender of the predators" manages to avoid a piece of liver. Only then will the reindeer be found untouched (Ravila 1934: 51–57).

This ritual of the desperate looking efforts of a defenseless undressed man in the freezing cold trying to reach the fire and obtain food and be faster than the reindeer herders, does not convey the impression of an equal or friendly attitude toward the predators. Predators are purposely represented as helpless; the "defender of the predators" is finally without any real chance of winning. The ritual confirms the role of men as the dominant power over predators.

In conclusion, ecological sustainability from the human point of view consists of two aspects: not bothering or disturbing the ecosystem so as not to reduce the possibilities of future use and so as to improve the well-being of living beings. Humans, animals and plants are bound together in a

---

58 The words used are in Inari Sámi and correspond to Northern Sámi "soahti" and "vašálaš."

network of reciprocity. Components are obliged to cooperate and support each other. Conflict and mutual hunting are aspects of the relationship. A feeling of safety is created.

As a constituent of the belief in generalized non-human personhood, a number of actions implying superhuman agency that have ecological sustainability as their aim then enter into force. Communication with animals, permission and other rituals, contract-like agreements on mutual rights and obligations accompanied by a sanction system enforced by spirits – all these are considered, at least by my informants, as fundamental instruments in shaping ecologically sustainable relationships with animals and plants in local ecosystems.

The belief in non-personhood creates patterns of identification and empathy with animals, plants and other surrounding entities. They are no longer alien nor dangerous but "beings" just like humans: they become like our children, friends and relatives with their own inherent dynamics and value. Animals, trees, stones and drums are regarded as having feelings, to be helping and sensitive like humans, and contribute to making humans happy.

Combined with the long-term and intergenerational strategy of survival and the total dependency on local resources, the identification and interdependent network of mutual relations between human and non-human persons create a powerful motivation to protect and strengthen the overall sustainable functioning of local ecosystems.

4.3 Individual Sacred Animals

In addition to being considered the equivalent of human beings, some ancient missionary sources explicitly confirm that the Sámi consider all animals to be sacred.[59]

> Within the traditional herding culture all wild animals and all living animals were holy. Certain ceremonies and strict rules were linked to the hunt. These rules had as purpose that the populations would be safeguarded (...) concrete punishment

---

59 "Man höll alla djur för heliga men björnen ansåg man som den allra heligasta." [One held all animals to be sacred, but the bear was the most sacred of all] I følge Randulf in Southern Sámi area, quoted by Bäckman (1975: 48).

measures could strike those that did not take into account the well-being of animals (Magga, Oskal & Sara 2001: 5).[60]

It is interesting that Magga et al. here underscore that all animals were considered sacred in the traditional herding culture and that this was linked to an ecologically sustainability function. Sometimes individual animals are especially sacred. As to the individual sacred animals, I received information through oral communication that those individual sacred animals should not be killed. I heard from two Sámi, one being Laila Spik, that a religious awareness can suddenly don on a hunter that the animal he is about to kill is sacred. For instance it might look the hunter straight intthe eye, this then inducing a certain religious state in the hunter. One of my respondents had himself experienced it. Laila Spik commented on this type of event as follows:

> One does not kill the sacred hare, it could be an important male necessary to providing important genes to the local hare population. Or a deceased relative of yours (LS Aug. 2012).

This remark of Laila Spik on the genetic importance of certain individuals to the larger population of a species in a certain area is significant. Sámi were traditionally highly aware of the way genetic selection in humans and animals functions and knew that strong individuals were vital to maintaining the most vital animal population possible. For instance they made keen observations regarding their reindeer herds and had to decide which male calves and bulls they would be castrating (to use in pulling sledges) or slaughtering so as to keep the best males in the flock for future reproduction. They also noticed that human offspring received properties from its ancestors, and they understood that animal reproduction functions according to the same logic (LS May 2013).

What could be the underlying sustainable logic of sacred individuals? It certainly is rule-affirming in the sense that religious experiences can regulate behavior in the hunt. First of all, meeting a sacred animal and respecting the interdiction to hunt reaffirms that the hunter must respect those rules and

---

60 Innen den tradisjonelle veidekulturen var alt vilt og alle levende dyr hellig. Visse seremonier og strenge regler var *knyttet til jakten. Disse regler hadde som hensikt dels at bestandene skulle bevares og dels at hvert enkelt dyr skulle respekteres (...)* Konkrete straffe mekanismer kunne ramme den som ikke tok hensyn til dyres vel og ve (Magga, Oskal & Sara 2001: 5).

gives him or her certainty that nature will comply and respect the rule that should provide enough food for rule-abiding humans. Second, as in most encounters with the sacred, it lends important meaning to the experience and gives that animal the status of a highly valuable being. A possibly sacred hare may possess a special ecological function that makes it too important to the local ecological balance to be killed. Finally this shows the closeness of humans and animals, their mutual identification and interchangeability, since they can reincarnate into each other: an ancestor can be reborn as an animal.

Chapter 5 – Species-Related Superhuman Agency

5.1 The Bear

The bear was considered the most sacred animal. He had a separate position in the ancient Sámi religion as the "landlord over all other animals in the forest" (Rheen quoted in Mebius 2007: 96).[61] The bear was the most powerful animal and seen as an ancestor of humans, as there are several traditional stories about Sámi women marrying friendly male bears and having human looking children (Kulonen 2005: 33, Fjellström 1755/1981: 14–15, Helander-Renvall 2010: 52). Human marriages could be consummated on bearskins (Holmberg 1915/1987: 41). Humans and bears had friendly relations that were very different from the relationship with other predatory animals. Bear hunts and disposal of the slain bear and the special way of burying its skeleton after being eaten – these were linked to special rituals.

The god *Leibolmai*, god of nature and the hunt, was related to the bear, was called "bear man" in certain traditions but not in others (Mebius 2007: 96–101). The bear rituals are frequently discussed in ancient missionary and comparative scholarly texts (Rydving 2010 compared Sámi and Khanty bear rituals). In 1755 in Lycksele, priest and teacher Pehr Fjellström published the description of a bear ritual in all its details which was republished with a comment by Louise Bäckman in 1981. Elina Helander-Renvall has discussed the role of the bear from a Sámi perspective (2010: 50–52).

Missionary Skanke reports that Sámi believe no meat tastes as good as bear meat and that this animal was sacred and a relative to humans:

> It is the opinion of these people that the bear (…) has a high intelligence and, as one says in some places in Norway, has the strength of ten men and the intelligence of twelve; therefore they consider the bear to be a member of humankind (Jessen-Schardebøll quoted in Rydving 1995: 172).[62]

---

61 "(…) huusbonde öfwer alla andra diur i skogen" (Rheen quoted in Mebius 2007: 96).

62 "Det er desuden disse Folkets Meening, at Biørnen (…), haver en sædeles høy Forstand, enn som man på sine Steder i Norge sier, haver Ti Mænds Styrke og

Yngve Ryd (1952–2012), the Swedish writer who had dedicated himself to writing down tje oral traditions of an elderly Sámi from the Jokkmokk area, has recorded a story about how Sámi families could have long-term friendly relationships with specific bear families.

Sámi children and bear cubs used to play children's games in absence of human adults. Only the bear parents would watch them. The ninety-year-old Sámi told Yngve Ryd (Ryd 2010) that humans could not attack those bears which they had befriended. Kuoljok Eidlitz (1999: 74) mentions that Lars Pirak (1932–2008), the well-known Sámi artist, had a relative who considered a bear to be a member of his family. Bäckman concludes from the Fjellström text that the attitude of the hunter was characterized by respect for a being of equal value that also had a soul and could think like humans (Bäckman in Fjellström 1981: 47).

The Swedish historian of religions Carl Martin Edsman (1911–2010) states that the bear can offer himself as prey to the hunter (Mebius 2007: 103). Laila Spik confirmed this with her own ritual practice of convincing a bear to accept his being slain. She told me in an interview that the bear is especially sacred and that eating his meat is a religious experience.[63] She also confirmed that she had heard that some Sámi children used to play with bear cubs in the old days. Even if the bear hunting is practically performed by a relative, she tries to enter into communication with the bear so as to "persuade the bear to accept being hunted." She also collects all the bear bones and buries them in a ceremonial way (LS Aug. 2012).

The aim of the ritual of the bear hunt is still being discussed. Some state that its aim is to make the bear tell other bears that they were treated respectfully by humans and did not have to be afraid of them (Bäckman in Fjellström 1981: 23). There is not detailed explanation as to what the role of ruler or manager of the landscape and all animals means. I found only one reference of Siv Norlander-Unsgaard that points to a role in ecology: she describes the bears' "central point of life-giving force for flora, fauna and homo sapiens," and that the bear ceremonies made people "wise and healthy" (quoted in Helander 2010: 51).

Tolv Mænds Vid; derover holde de for, at Biørnen bør regnes til det menneskelige Kiøn" (Jessen-Schardebøll quoted in Rydving 1995: 172).

63 This is also mentioned by L. Bäckman (1991: 20).

The relationship with the bear shows important principles which are important for ensuring ecologically sustainable relationships with the ecosystems. First, humans share a hybrid identity with the bear since it is seen as their mythological ancestor which might in some cases have married human females. This results in identification and empathy. Second, the bear clearly has personhood and is seen as an autonomous conscious being, which again results in identification and empathy. Third, the bear is not primarily considered a dangerous predator but is treated on an equal basis with humans and can be their personal friend. Fourth, the bear is a sacred animal, which might help humans because granting them wisdom and strength from the contact with the bear. It gives meaning and identity to people who eat bear meat, hunt the bear and perform rituals. Fifth, it has some kind of sacred power as a life-giving force to the landscape, according to one source that does not elaborate much on this aspect.

5.2 Animal Species-Related Protection Spirits: The *Máddo*[64]

The *máddo* (origin or root in Northern Sámi) or *species+eadni* (*mother of + species*) can be considered one of the central elements in understanding the way that Sámi traditional religion dealt with ecological sustainability regarding attitudes and behavior toward animals. The most sacred animal species were bear, reindeer and perhaps salmon.[65] They have a special status and are not mentioned as having *máddo*. I discussed the bear in chapter 5.1 and the reindeer in chapter 7.2. The *máddo* tradition has been mostly described by sources with a Sámi perspective since the beginning of the twentieth century – by people like Johan Turi (1910, 1920) and in the stories told to Qvigstad (published 1926–1928). There they figure next to stories about the

---

64 See appendixes to this chapter with the overview of máddo stories and newly recorded stories.

65 As to the salmon, I have only one story about a ritual related to that species. It was usual in the Tana area to cook a special first-salmon soup made of the first salmon caught normally in May, after breakup of the ice on the Tana River. This soup was shared in a feast with the local community. The soup was special since it had a special and appreciated taste, including both the head and tail of the salmon, which are normally removed when making salmon soup (information from a local traditional salmon fisherman Raidar Varsi, April 2013). See also Hultkrantz (1994: 359) which describes the Tana River's first salmon ritual.

underground people and *noaidi* and other superhuman beings and are apparently considered to be important to them. In the appendix is a schematic overview of all *máddo* stories I found.

Genii species play a role in maintenance of a system that regulates behavior by prohibiting overharvesting and which limits any disturbance of living conditions for animal populations. The genii species establishes a framework for values and attitudes of respect and regarding an inherent right to live well for every species, even the most insignificant for human use.

The species-related protection spirits were not actively worshipped and did not receive any offerings. When they intervened, their action was punitive. They have been described as a type of "bogey" phenomenon that was part of the world of childrearing (Pentikäinen 1997: 226). As this research will show, many traditional-thinking Sámi still consider them as a part of the adult world. The *máddo* is still an element of the present-day Sámi tradition. References and stories about them can be found in sources from Northern, Lule, Inari and Skolt Sámi. The Southern Sámi tradition has not been researched. For this analysis an attempt was made to gather a representative selection of *máddo* stories from different Sámi areas. As to the terminology used in this paper, I will employ the term that scholars who have written about this issue have used, namely a guardian spirit of species (Paulson 1961) or genius speciei. This term *spirit* is not used for the species-related animal protection spirits in any of the sources about by Sámi themselves, even if they have a term for it: *vuoinga*.

What Is a *Máddo*[66]?

"Juokke diŋas læ mád'do" (everything has a *máddo*) says the first line of a story recorded in Kautokeino (Qvigstad 1928 II: 474). Traditional stories from various Northern and Lule areas repeat the belief that every species had its own leading protection and/or ancestor spirit (Qvigstad 1927 I: 416, Andersen 2005: 72, interviews Sigvald Persen and Solveig Tangeraas Feb. 2012). Itkonen, the source for Inari Sámi, explicitly mentions that *máddos* were only known for three named types of fish and not for three other named

---

66 In some sources the word is written with a 'u' at the end, in other 'o'. "Máddo" is the contemporary Northern Sámi spelling.

fish species. Kulonen, referring to Itkonen and Pentikäinen, says that *máddu* is a fish protection spirit and *cubbomáddu* is the protective spirit for frogs (Kulonen 2005: 213).

The guardian spirit dwells in the same place as the individuals of the species they protect. They do not move away from them to any other places. It is very characteristic that they always have the same appearance as the animal concerned. At the same time, they are substantially larger and stronger, even whale-sized, than the individuals of the species protected. The frog-*máddo* is described as the size of a man or cat. Sea animal *máddos* are huge monsters. Some fish *máddos* are known to have horns, as the pike *máddo* has been described (Itkonen 1946: 105–6).

The protection spirits require respect in the form of a strict set of rules for right attitudes and behavior. In the case of fish, overfishing is often mentioned as a form of unacceptable behavior,[67] as is any other form of mistreatment and poaching or grumbling about the fish catch (Kulonen 2005: 213). It also includes impolite comments like saying that the fish is ugly or too skinny (Itkonen 1946) or in making any unnecessary sounds, disturbing the habitat even just by turning over stones, and causing all forms of unnecessary physical discomfort or pain to animals. If these rules are transgressed in a serious manner, the spirits would apply, often without any forewarning, severe punishments.

The animal-species protection spirit was powerful and therefore deeply feared. Its punishments were extremely severe: absence or loss of catch, physical attack, illness, often death of the transgressor. There is only one example where the fish mother helps people. According to that story the foremother of all fish can appear as ball of fire in the dark time and move over the ocean, and the strength and direction of the light ball gives information as to the amount of fish and the direction they come from that year (Kalstad 197: 25)

(Andersen 2005). They were not subject to any form of permisssion ritual or worship, like sacrifice, and were not even greeted when one would pass by a place where they were known to be living.

---

67 "Dersom man tok opp for mye uer kunne man bli utsatt for háhkkamáddos vrede." [If one took too much fish, one could become exposed to revenge of the háhkamáddo.] (Andersen 2005)

Máddo Terminology

The species-related protection spirit could have various names. The most frequently used name is *máddo*. Some sources call them *animal species name + eadni* (mother), like cubbo-eadni (Turi 2012/1910: 127) or (*oldest of*) (Qvigstad I-579). In Norwegian sources it can be called *stammor* (foremother), *åndelig overhode* (spiritual master), *beskyttelsesånd* (protection spirit) (Andersen 2005).

There seem to be at least four different Sámi words for the concept of the species-related guardian spirit. *Máddo* comes from the Northern Sámi word *máddu* meaning "origin" or "root," like of trees. In Northern Sámi, *máddo* is the general term for this type of spirit used in Northern and Lule Sámi coastal areas for all types of land and water animals (Kalstad 1997, Andersen 2005). Johan Turi, who lived at Karesuando and in the Swedish/Norwegian mountains, never mentions the term *máddo*. He uses the term *eadni* (mother) for the bird-mosquito-frog guardian spirit he tells stories about. Qvigstad has recorded the use of *cubbomáddo* as far inland as Kautokeino (Qvigstad II 1928: 474). Itkonen uses the term *máddu* in his research concerning the Inari Sámi only for fish species. Birds have a *bird mother* and other categories of animals have an *eatni* or a *halde* (Itkonen 1946: 115). In my interviews and visits in Porsanger, Karasjok and Tana, *máddos* for frogs, mice, squirrels, snow grouse and fish were known to be spoken about.

The bird-mother is called *loddsen akka* by Skolt Sámi and *loddis aedne* by Inari Sámi, as quoted by Itkonen (1946: 80) and Paulson (1961: 143). She protects local and migratory birds that travel to her in the autumn.

A reindeer-woman *luohtt-hozjik*, or "mistress of the wilderness" related to the Russian word for *hozjain* meaning "landlord" or "master" in the Inari area is mentioned by Itkonen as a reindeer guardian spirit (1946: 78). She and a more specific *pots-hozjin* "reindeer-mistress" is also mentioned for Kola Sámi (Paulson 1961: 142). There are several reindeer and wolf protection spirits from the Kola Peninsula. The wolf protector is said to take revenge if one kills too many wolves (Paulson 1961: 142).

For mosquitoes, frogs, and birds the term *eadni* is used instead of the term *máddo* by Turi (1910 and 1920). In one *máddo*-like story of Qvigstad from Kautokeino the term "hui stuora cuobbo" (very big frog) is used (Qvigstad II 1927: 476).

Kulonen ea (2005: 213) has an entry on *máddu* called the "oldest of fish." Using the oldest sources of Turi and Itkonen, one could conclude that *máddo* is most used for creatures like seafish and freshwater dwellers and other water animals such as lobster, squid and frogs. "Species name+*eadni*" is used for insects and birds.

Fellman used the term *halde* for the beaver, bear, wolf and fish individual and also species-related protection spirits (quoted in Bäckman 1969: 132, Paulson 1961: 142). *Háldi* seems to be the term used for mammal exept the reindeer. The *háldi* term connects the *genius speciei* to a different type of spirit: the local managing spirit such as a *sieidi* (see the text about *sieidi)*.

How to explain this variability? One possible explanation is that the more early and vigorously Norwegianized areas of the coastal Northern and Lule Sámi – including the Kautokeino Sámi from the Qvigstad who have their summer grazing lands on the fjords coasts – have simply generalized the term *máddo* that might have been related not only to water creatures but to all other animals, while the more "unsullied" Sámi populations in the inlands have kept some kind of ancient and more nuanced terminology. In my opinion, based on the sparse materials that we have, it is important to remain cautious before drawing too strict conclusions about a more ancient use of the term. They all come from a period in which this knowledge was still very much taboo and hidden. Itkonen does not elaborate much on the species-related protection spirits. He only has a few lines about each of them.

Scholars on Species-Related Protection Spirits

The *máddo* or mother type of species-related protection spirits are with the exception of Ivar Paulson a relatively minor theme and are not seen as a distinct category for many scholars with a non-Sámi perspective writing on Sámi religion in the twentieth century. Several scholars tried to show overlap and similarities between various types of spirits and tried to reduce them to a common basic identity in which they are variations of ancestor spirits, or to a myriad of fluctuating unstable types of spirits that they declare to be so chaotic that it is impossible to be further categorized. Many either failed to mention the *máddo* type or, if mentioned, they did not go into depth as to what the *máddo*'s ecological functions were. For the aim of this study, it is interesting to deepen the properties and functions of both categories and to highlight their differences.

Máddo-type spirits are often seen as identical with the *háldi*, a kind of ownership-related protection spirit. *Háldi* is related to the word of ruling, owning, mastering and, in modern Sámi, managing (Bäckman 1975: 129–130). The word *háldi* is also a term linked to subterranean spirits, and older research before World War II it was connected to a belief in ancestors; however, now it is declared to have more diverse origins, like representing animal species or limited areas of the landscape (Bäckman 1975: 130, 132).

Holmberg (1915/1987) does describe various names for individual female protection spirits that were found in nature. As to animal species-related spirits, he writes only about the mother of the birds and does not mention the term *máddo* or protective spirits for animal species (Holmberg 1915/1987: 76–78).

Ivar Paulson (1961) has systematically described species-related guardian spirits of the "origin" or "mother"-type for the Sámi cultural context. Paulson elaborated important categories,: "a species-related spirit can often be considered as protector and owner of all individuals of his animal species" (Paulson 1961: 142).[68] He was aware that distinctions between guardian-type spirits and owner-type spirits can be difficult to make because functions can overlap. Paulson believed that nature-spirits have grown together with species-related spirits to form complex representations (1961: 141). For instance fish-spirits could be of the local ownership-type of spirits and be linked to the belief in *sáivo*, which is the term for the sacred places, mostly mountains, where certain ancestors live and also for the ancestors themselves (Paulson 1961: 146). They sometimes have the same name as the species-related guardian spirits, and here he refers to the *háldi* we find at Fellman (Paulson 1961). Paulson also underscores that the species-related spirits concern species which are hunted and he does not quote any source suggesting the belief that all animal species have their own *genius speciei*. In his conclusion Paulson enters a plea for more archival research so as to clarify these issues (1961: 148).

Louise Bäckman does not elaborate on the distinction between an ownership or management type of animal spirit and the *máddo*. She has focused on animal-related protection spirits in her 1991 article "The Master of the

---

68 "...da ein Artgeist zumeist auch für alle Einzeltiere seiner Tierart als Beschützer und Eigner gilt" (Paulson 1961: 141).

Animal." Here she elaborates on the ownership type that she relates to the bear, *sieidis*, *Storjuncker* and the *noaidi*. Her point is that she sees them as autonomous and not as a form of further development of the worship of ancestors. The word *máddo* is only referred to exist in Skolt-Sámi culture in Bäckman's text with respect to the *sáivo* spirits (1975: 133). She quotes for instance Arbman, and the eighteenth century missionaries J. Kildal and Randulf, to state that the protectors of the animals had an autonomous role in *sáivo* (1975: 135). They can be a part of the *sáivo* spirits and become a guardian of the *noaidi*. "It can be true that the protection spirit of the *noaidi* is recruited from the protection spirits of animal species (1975: 134) (Bäckman 1975: 132–133).[69] Otherwise the animal species spirits are ranged under the overarching denomination of *háldi*. For her, the *háldi* or "master of" a species or type of animal rules over the hunting results and negotiates with humans – it needs to be negotiated with and sacrificed to. "The háldi is of utmost importance as an economical guarantee, and it was important to treat them in the right way" (Bäckman 1975: 135).[70] Bäckman writes that clear distinctions can be difficult to make, as with religious change, various types of spirit beings merged with one another (1975: 134, 138).

In his 1994 text "Religion and Environment among the Saami," Åke Hultkranz mentions a few of the mother type of species-related spirits: the mother of birds, the reindeer mother *Tshorve edne* (horn mother). He does not use the word *máddo* nor does he mention that every species was considered as having a "mother" His perspective on animal species-related spirits remains utilitarian: "A list of all these animal spirits indicates which animals have been important to the Saami, either because of their value as food or because of their dangerous aspects" (1994: 360). For Hultkrantz the "masters of animals" spirits are always related to the purpose of achieving good hunting results and are therefore uniquely associated with human survival (Hultkrantz 1994: 360).

---

69 "Det kan vara riktigt, ty noajdiens tjänste- och hjälpväsen rekryterades troligen ur djurarterna skyddsväsen." (Bäckman 1975: 134.)

70 „Halderna hade stor betydelse som ekonomiske garanter, vilka det var viktigt att rätt umgås med." (Bäckman1975: 135.)

Nor does Hans Mebius elaborate on typologies and the concepts of nature and animal-related spirits. He does not mention the word *máddo* of *mother of + a species* in his book *Bissie* (2007) which gives an otherwise rather extensive overview of the ancient Sámi religion. Mebius cites "djurens rådare" (the ruler of the animals) as being mentioned by the missionary Skanke (Mebius 2007: 89). He briefly discusses the "olika skrämselväsen om vilka det berättas i samisk folktro" (different bogey spirits Sámi popular beliefs tell about) (Mebius 2007: 142). They are viewed in relation to what he sees as a fear for animals, which according to him is a characteristic of the ambiguous relationship between hunter and its prey (Holmberg-Harva by Mebius 2007: 103). Besides fear there can simultaneously be sympathy for animals, he records (H.-J. R. Paproth quoted in Mebius 2007: 103).

Pentikäinen describes the *máddo* in his category of protection spirits in a short paragraph as children's bogey spirits and focuses on the frightening and imposing restrictions and punishments. He proposes the possibility that they were transformed into being bogey spirits only for children in the current of time, and he considers the possibility that they could have been imagined only for that purpose (1997: 226). Pentikäinen made the observation that the Sámi did not sacrifice or devote complicated ceremonies to the "nature spirits."[71]

Pentikäinen discusses in one paragraph (1997: 224) how protection spirits have a normative and value-enforcing role toward places, flora and fauna, without explaining what values and norms are concerned. He mentions that those spirits when properly treated can help people and thus provide security. None of these scholars discuss their role as a motivating force for respectful treatment of animals and as regulators of the ecologically sustainable use of resources.

Modern oral sources that tell of living traditions have been written down in more recent decades and have helped to differentiate roles and to deepen understanding of their various aspects. Scholars writing from a Sámi perspective,

---

71 "Die Saamen opferten diesen Gestalten nicht und zelebrierten auch keine aufwendigen Rituale zu ihren Ehren." (The Sámi did not make offerings to them and neither did they celebrate any complicated rituals for them.) (Pentikäinen 1997: 221.)

like Kalstad (1997), Andersen (2005) and Ole Henrik Magga (2001, 2011) mention the *máddo* explicitly as a separate category and designate it as a key motivating force for respectful behavior toward animals and concern with environmental protection. They confer strong significance to the *máddo* in the contemporary discussions about animal welfare and protection of the environment. For them it shows that Sámi have strong traditional values in terms of protecting animals, these values linked to a different perspective on the term "nature" and animal protection and nature conservation.

In conclusion, in terms of the scholarly debate, one can say that the species-related protection spirits of the *máddo* type, with basically a female and non-utilitarian and autonomous role, has only been taken up by scholars with a Sámi perspective.

Older Animal-Species Protection-Spirit Stories (1880–1920)

Johan Turi has taken down stories about the mother of frogs, *cubbo eadni* (2011: 127) and the mother of mosquitoes (1920: 217). The mother of the mosquitoes, *čuoika ädni*, figures in a story called "The Mosquitoes in the Olden Time," which relates how the mosquitoes came to the Sámi lands. At first there were no mosquitoes in the Sámi lands. They were told by the spider, who was there first, that it was a wonderful place. The mother of the mosquitoes decided that a few mosquitoes should travel there to explore the Sámi lands. Many of them perished, for instance drowned in milk pots. When the remaining ones returned, the mother of the mosquitoes decided that she did not want any more mosquitoes going to the Sámi lands. She considered it too dangerous for them. The mosquitoes, however, did not obey their mosquito-mother and decided that the Sámi lands would not be dangerous if they all went together. And so they did. The mother of frogs, described by Johan Turi, kills an adult woman because she had tortured frogs many years before when she was still a child (2011: 127).

Isak Saba (1875–1921), the first Sámi to become a member of the national parliament and composer of the Sámi national anthem, and originating from the eastern part of the Northern Sámi coastal area, mentions in a slightly humorous vein just how big in fact was the original ancestor of the haddock, "hysens opphav." It looked like an extremely large fish and "took a whole day in the dark time before it had swum past someone who stood on the beach."[72] In the dark time there is no day, so the huge animal probably did not exist (Saba, quoted by Magga, Oskal & Sara 2001: 8).

Qvigstad has recorded stories about frogs, sea creatures, beetles and mice. In one story a frog *máddo* scares a child who tortures frogs. It bites the leg off a child that has tortured the local frog population over a long period of time, and the child is crippled forever (Qvigstad IV 1929: 329–331). It is said that dung beetles (a large scarabee-type of black beetle) when unnecessarily killed by a Sámi just for crawling over his belongings, will in revenge then suck blood from people and kill them by causing disease with ther bites (Qvigstad II 1928: 476). As for the mouse *máddo*, the punishment for behaving disrespectfully toward mice, for example killing them, is that the more mice a person kills the more mice will arise and bite and cling to you by the hundreds and kill you in the end (Qvigstad II 1928: 477).

Qvigstad has published a story for North-Troms about squid fishers that had been harvesting a huge amount of animals. The storyteller remembers that he went fishing with his father, when they saw fire under their boat. The fire was interpreted as a sign announcing the coming of the *máddo*. They immediately stopped fishing and returned straight home (Andersen 2005: 73, Qvigstad 1928: 475–477).

In Itkonens text, *máddo* always refers to fish. Many fish species have a *guolle-máddu* (fish *máddo*), like the ones that were used as food: "Hávga" (pike), "vuoskon" (perch), "dápmot" (trout) and "tsuovdzam" (lake whitefish). Three less edible types of inland fish are mentioned not to have a *máddo*.[73] The pike *máddo* has two horns that point backward. With these it can make holes in fishermen's nets and thus allowing the fish to escape. This can happen if a fisherman mistreats fish or even only verbally criticizes them for being too thin. The other *máddo*, without horns, can also make holes in nets. If fish disappear from nets, one says that the *máddo* has taken or eaten them. The *máddo* does not just take fish away from the net but "eats" them. Itkonen tells the story of a frog *máddo* that comes out of the water and bites children's feet when they mistreat a frog or put frog eggs on land (Itkonen 1946: 106). Ravila tells how children are threatened with

---

72 "Det gikk en hel dag i mørketiden innen den svøm for en som stå på stranden" (Saba, quoted by Magga, Oskal & Sara 2001: 8).
73 Burbot, grayling, one unknown species.

a frog *máddo tsubbomáddu* which emerges from the water and devours them if they come too close to the lake (Ravila 1934: 115).

There are no stories recorded of any sacrifice or rituals for asking permission from species-related spirits. The *kuli-hälde* or fish-spirit mentioned at Itkonen receives a sacrifice to facilitate the fishing, while the *fishmáddo* in the same text does not (1946: 104).[74]

Contemporary *Máddo* Stories (1920–Now)

Animal species-related protection spirits are remembered and transmitted in oral tradition today in many places, like the Norwegian coast to the Lule-Sámi area of Tysfjord and the Northern Sámi inlands. The Sámi researcher Oddmund Andersen, from the Árran center i Tysfjord, has gathered a number of local, oral and contemporary Lule-Sámi stories about *máddo*, and he quotes several of them that were broadcast over the radio in the last fifteen years (Andersen 2005). Most *máddo* stories are about separate species. There are a few stories about a generalized animal-type, like the *guollemáddo* for all fish (Andersen 2005: 72).

From Tysfjord in the Lule-Sámi area there are *máddo* stories about three sea creatures: lobster, octopus and redfish. A story by Inger Karlsen (Andersen 2005) tells of a squid fisherman who used to sing and shout when out fishing alone in the sea. One day the other fishermen found his boat reversed and the fisherman missing at the exact place they knew the squid *máddo* was living. The other fishermen concluded that the *máddo* might have done that to stop him from making too much noise on the sea. There are two stories about sea fishermen who decide to return immediately from the fishing when they notice that the fishing lines do not sink downward as they should. The sea suddenly seems shallow where it should not be. This can be a warning signal that a

---

74 There is a spirit called "skaimadas," which translates as "water spirit" by Itkonen and which receives an offering of bird meat (Itkonen 1946: 105). The "-madas" ending in the name is of unknown etymology according to the Sámi language expert Prof. Pekka Sammallahtti, and is most likely not related to the word *máddo*. The Northern Inari Sámi dialect from which this word seemingly stems, was the language of the person who was probably the main informant of Itkonen, the one-eyed reindeer herder Johan Nuorgam. This language has died out (Facebook conversation in April 2013, quoted with permission of the author).

life-threatening *máddo* is shortly to arrive. The same lady also knew a story about the lobster *máddo*. Someone had seen it in the shape of a huge lobster.

Máddo stories from the Johan Albert Kalstad texts, which he collected from many different sources without any direct reference, are not dated. As to my own interviews, it was surprising to note that almost every Sámi speaker – namely between the ages of 50 and 70 from the Northern Sámi inner areas in Finnmark to whom I mentioned the *máddo* – knew a story from their childhood that they were eager to tell me.[75] From Porsanger, a Western North Sámi area, I have recorded three contemporary *máddo* stories from S. Persen and Solveig Tangeraas. Sigvald Persen from Stabbursnes tells the story of the local family that avoided a drinking well over many years because of a frog *máddo* they believed to live there. They preferred to walk a long distance to another well so as not to meet that *máddo*. Sigvald Persen also relates that according to the oral traditions of his area all animals have a *máddo*. He underscores how extremely scared people were of the *máddo*: "If you met a *máddo*, you had done something wrong. People could not take the slightest risk in meeting a *máddo*" (SP Feb. 2013).

Solveig Tangeraas' stories show that Solveig as a child knew exactly what a *máddo* was and was also aware of the fact that every animal species had one. She knew that one had to be afraid of that and react immediately in the cast that it should suddenly appear. She confirms the rule that animals should not be disturbed or moved and that any transgression of that rule implies a punishment. The *máddo*-belief prevents children and adults from disturbing animals even in very subtle ways and causes them to avoid walking through or to certain places so as not to meet the *máddo*.

Olaf, another local informant from a village a bit further north in the fjord, who was ignorant of the Sámi language, did not remember having heard any *máddo* story. One elderly local fisherman in the Tana area confirmed, with some emotion in his voice, that he had become acquainted with the *máddo* of fish when he was a six-year-old taken out to learn

---

75 Two of those stories, one by Asta Balto and one about Johan Jernsletten, are in the appendix.

fishing in inland lakes by his grandfather (man living in Valjohka, oral communication April 2013).

Ecological Sustainability: Role of the *Máddo* Guardian Spirits

The stories about the specific species-protection spirits, like the *máddo* and "*mother of-*" story tradition have a clear role in maintaining a value and behavioral system that aims at maintaining a sustainable relationship with the local populations of animal species. Their influence on value and behavior can be differentiated into four aspects: 1) in the interpretation of the various terms for the genius species; 2) the analysis of the categories of animals that stories have been recorded and their frequency; 3) the incentives for influencing concrete behavior; 4) the type of relationship between humans and animals that is reflected by this type of species-related guardian spirit system.

Sustainability and the Interpretation of the Terminology

The significance of the word *máddo* corresponds to the word *eadni,* since they both have the dimension of "origin" as their key aspect. The word *eadni* can be interpreted as having a stronger focus on protection and caretaking, while the term *máddo* is purely focused on the origin. Concern for the origin can be biologically seen as a focus on the reproduction rate of the stock.

Could the term *máddo* possibly be an original term for water-related protection spirits of an entire a species, as we did not find any designation of an *eadni* for fish (Kulonen 2005)? It may be true that water creatures live mostly undisturbed until they are caught, while land animals have to confront many sorts of potential human disturbance throughout their lifetime. Can a possible explanation be that the potential reproductive rate for water animals is mostly dependent on how many of them are taken out by humans, while food supplies and other essential elements of their living conditions are more or less out of the danger zone of human interference? While for land animals like frogs that whole-life disturbance factor by humans is more important, might the term *eadni* be used in the sense that they need more "care"?

The term *halde* referring to guarding or managing has again an even stronger focus on the aspect of the management of life. In Itkonen *halde* is used for various types of local and animal spirits. Can it be that the mammals that have *halde* have an even stronger potential for being disturbed by humans than birds and insects and that protection during the whole of their lifetime takes on an even stronger focus? This use of names needs more field-work to find out if the term *eadni* is still in use for instance in the Inari area.

Sustainability Issue in the Frequency and Selection of Stories about Species

The available guardian-spirit stories can be divied into four types of animal species. The first category regards species that are used for the basic food supply and do not have fragile populations, like cod or haddock. Here there is almost a complete lack of stories. The second category is species that are harvested as a food resource or otherwise are important for human life and do have fragile populations that might therefore require careful harvesting and protection. They are frogs, squid, lobster, snow grouse, redfish and inland fishes. There are many stories told about them. The third category is those that are not hunted by humans and do not have any direct use but live close to humans and are fragile and easy targets to harm. It can be many species of birds, insects, mice or lemming. They are represented in numerous stories. A fourth category is predatory animals like wolf, bear, fox and otter. There we only have sparse mentions of the existence and of names of protective spirits.

As to the species that are fragile and are of interest for human use, most widespread and generally most elaborated are the stories about frogs.

Frogs are dependent on small and often shallow ponds where they have high visibility. A frog is easily caught and its eggs can easily be removed. It is easy to exterminate or substantially diminish a frog population in a pond. Frogs were important for traditional medical use, their slime was used to heal burns (MM April 2013) and they kept drinking wells clean from in-sects, plants and other dirt (ST May 2013). At the same time one can hardly imagine a more tempting species for children to play with. Using a pond or well where frogs live to fetch water on a daily basis cannot but disturb the frog population. An other fragile spiecies is the lobster. Lobsters are known to be relatively few and overfishing can easily reduce stock over a longer time. They are strongly protected today and their fishing is heavily regulated. And squid have a special and unexplained life cycle in Norwegian seas. They appear and disappear in periods and can be almost absent for many years. When squid return, they can appear at local spots in great numbers at once.

Redfish are also relatively rare fish. Inland lake fish stocks can easily be depleted when overfished.[76] For inland lake fish there was and still is at some places a traditional intensive human regulation system in place as the lakes could easily be emptied of the best edible fish. The lake then became unusable for supplying food for a decades or even forever. Inland lake fish stocks had to be actively maintained by fishing in order to remain usable and strong. The right amount of outtake of fish was necessary so that the remaining fish did not get too small and too weak. Predator fish were also kept actively at a low level. Each of my informants confirmed the existence of this traditional management system. They all had angry stories about lakes emptied by ignorant intruders. In the list of freshwater fish-*máddos* from Itkonen I found detailed information about inland lake fish. The two tastiest inland fish species, Arctic char and trout, are strangely enough missing.

There are a few detailed stories about predator guardian spirits. The fox-*máddo* tricks humans so that they do not get the fox, and the wolves punish those that hunt too many of them. There exist stories of how humans should behave ethically toward predators (Turi 2012/1910) but they do not involve the intermediate of a species-related guardian.

Mice, frogs, beetles, ants and lemmings are animals that come close to humans and that some might easily kill "for fun" or because they cause a small nuisance.

Most animals that are protected by a *máddo* or species-eadni are relatively small and feeble – small squids, frogs and so forth. Their *máddo* is strong and large and compensates for their tiny size. It might be concluded that stories of the guardian spirits take care of the animals that need it most, that are small and weak, like frogs, lobsters, mice and beetles and inland fish.

The stories about species that humans do not use seem to transmit a message of the inherent value of the animal. The mosquito story appears to be related to human activity: it gives an excuse to humans to be allowed to kill them. The mosquitoes are in the Sámi land against the will of their mother-spirit after she had clearly warned them about the deadly dangers. She might therefore not be able to protect them if they are killed. The story is coherent with the concept that animals have their own personality by showing how

---

76 Information from Store Norske Leksikon, online edition www.snl.no, read in
   March 2013.

mosquitoes make autonomous decisions as to where to live and what risks to take. It is interesting that Turi relates such an apologetic story about a tiny, insignificant animal.

It can be concluded that the species-related guardian spirits take care of the animals that need it most from both a human and an ecological perspective: the smaller and weaker ones that are used as food supply but have fragile populations, or the ones with no direct value that are prone to be killed by humans for no reason. There is a double logic here – on the one hand avoiding over-harvesting of food supplies and protecting clean drinking water, and a general protection of all types of animals.

A Well-Reflected Rule-Enforcing Role

The species-related guardian spirit system with its double aim of protecting harvesting potential for fragile species and protecting animals for their own inherent value has four key aspects for influencing human behavior and attitudes toward ecological sustainability. First, with its absolute authority of being able to severely punish transgression, it is preventive and educative. Second, it provides security with respect to food supplies and the support of surrounding animals to humans. A *máddo* does not attack without reason. If it does not appear, one is doing safe fishing, you are treating animals well, it means that the *máddo* will do its work and animal populations will reproduce and thrive. The heavy penalties that the *máddo* can impose have as paradoxical effect that they simultaneously provide a profound sensation of safety. Third, there is an element of attributing personhood to animals by designating an "animal mother" that is as caring for the animals as the human mother for the children. This seems to function very well as an attractive image, especially for children, who are very much aware of their dependence on their mother. An identification and empathy with animals is therefore created. And last, it also leads to reflection on the cultural meaning of this type of superhuman agency and creates awareness and discussion of the underlying objective needed to ensure that local animal populations are harvested in a sustainable manner and so as to safeguard their general well-being.

> It [the *máddo*, MB] has as task to guard the species it was "mother" for. Kalstad says that the idea was that everyone should show respect for the various types of animals and that self-limitation instead of greedyness was valorized. Mikael Urheim has the same point of view. (…) From a pedagogical perspective, the *máddo* tradition can

be considered as part of the raising of children and their socialization to the norms and values of society (Andersen 2005: 74).[77]

Sámi themselves seem to be very much aware of the role of ecologically sustainable values and behavior as well as of the máddo stories – and these extend into their adult lives. Some informants showed that the *máddo* was, without any problem, simultaneously understood as symbolic and literal. The superhuman reality could be explained and at the same time lived. They were clearly aware of the *máddo's* role in education, prevention and finally in imposing rules of behavior.

5.3 Animal Ancestry

Scholars such as Durkheim considered animal ancestry as the origin of religion and as having a profound impact on the way a person or a family perceives their relationship to the local natural environment (Harvey 2006: 12, quoting Rose). Even if some scholars seem to have revived its use (Harvey 2006 quotes Rose Århem and others) I prefer in this study not to use the term "totemism" because it might still be too closely associated with that discriminatory evolutionistic phase in the development of religious studies.

The motif of animal ancestry – with bears in Northern and Lule Sámi areas and reindeer in Skolt and Eastern Sámi culture – is related in ancient stories as well as in more recent ones on the arctic hare as a living oral tradition. The traditional stories about caring male bears having offspring with human women have been recorded on many occasions and places in the Skolt and Northern Sámi cultural areas (we examined this theme in the section on the bear). As to the reindeer, the Russian ethnologist Vladimir Charnoluski (1894–1969) visited Kola Peninsula in the late 1920s and recorded ancient beliefs and ancient tales and over thirty stories about the *Meandash*, the mythical reindeer ancestor-man. The worship of totems is

---

77 "Den (*máddo*, MB) hadde som oppgave å passe på den arten som den var «mor» for. Kalstad sier at ideen var at hver skulle vise respekt for de ulike dyreslag, der måtehold fremfor grådighet ble vektlagt. Den samme synspunkt hevder også Mikael Urheim. (...) På en pedagogisk synspunkt kan *máddo* tradisjonen betraktes som et ledd i barneoppdragelse og sosialisering til samfunnets normer og verdier" (Andersen 2005: 74).

said to be common at the time when Charnoluski made his expedition to the Kola Peninsula, "although for obvious reasons the local people were not overly eager to discuss it with strangers."[78] The *Meandash* in Eastern Sámi Kildin mythology is a reindeer that also is a man. He has a human mother and reindeer father. He takes on the appearance of a human and marries a Sámi female and they have human-looking children. They can be involuntarily turned back into animals if they do not respect certain rules.[79]

As to the more recent stories told by Sámi to researchers, Itkonen mentions the oral tradition of accompanying "family animal spirits" that are passed on from father to son and from mother to daughter in two villages concerning a number of Skolt Sámi families. They can appear in dreams. Their identity is only to be revealed when a young person turns twenty years old. The rule is that they cannot eat the meat of the respective animal. Itkonen related this type of spirit to what he calls the "totemic" tradition. Animal species mentioned are sheep, horse, cats, hawks, wild and tame reindeer, wolves, dogs, pike and others (Itkonen 1946: 163, 164). In contemporary Sámi culture it can be found in the form of animal species tracks used as characteristics or nicknames for a certain family (Pentikäinen 1997: 80–81). Pentikäinen does not specify the place or reference for this information.

A sea Sámi family that I visited within the framework of my research in the Tana area, a Sea Sámi area in Eastern Finnmark, Northern Norway, possesses an oral tradition which says that they are as a family related to

---

78 Estonian Literary Museum, www.folklore.ee/folklore/vol11/meandash.htm read on 05.04.2013). See also Pentikäinen 1997: 81–82 for Meandash stories and publication of Porsanger, Jelena 1994, 2000, and others.

79 A well known story from the Eastern Sámi goes as follows: Three sisters marry a reindeer, a raven and a seal. The reindeer is by far the best-suited husband of the three. Their children are human beings. Because the woman breaks a taboo that her husband had imposed on her by putting reindeer skins that were wetted by their children in the sunshine and not in a running stream, she and her children are turned into wild reindeer forever. According to this myth, that is the origin of wild reindeer. The reindeer learned to become game animals and sacrifice themselves to the humans because human were their relatives (Kulonen 2005: 216). For a systematic overview, see the Estonian folklore site http://www. folklore.ee/folklore/vol11/meandash.htm, that contains book references mainly to V. Charnoluski. Read on 28.10.2015.

the Arctic hare. The memory of that tradition stretches back to time immemorial. Besides the oral tradition, they respect a nearby sacred site with smaller stones on it and consider it to be sacred to that animal. For them it is of utmost importance that this sacred site is not disturbed in any way.

As to the implication for ecological sustainability of an ancestor relationship with an animal species, it is obvious that this generates a drastically different relationship to all animals in general and to the natural world as a whole. The boundaries between human and animal identity have become relative once more. How does one relate to an ancestor? With deeply felt identification, empathy and respect. Ancestors are seen as examples to follow, as key teachers and caretakers of their descendants. Knowledge and concern about living conditions of the animal species become key elements of the identity of each individual of that family. "Totemic relations connect people (human and other-than human) to their ecosystems in nonrandom relations of mutual care" (Debbie Rose and Kaj Århem quoted in Harvey 2006: 12, 166). This identification will serve as a powerful motivation to preserve the habitats and living conditions of that certain species and animals in general.

Chapter 6 – Local Superhuman Agency

6.1 Underground Spirits: Gufithar/Kadnihah/Ulda

Gufithar, kadnihah or *ulda* are the most widespread names in the different Sámi regions for what is seen by Sámi as a separate people of anthropomorphic superhuman beings. They can also be called *háldi*.

Háldi is related to the Finnish word "halti," which means to rule or protect (Bäckman 1975: 129–130). *Háldi* as a designation for the underground people is to be found in many stories, for example those recorded by Qvigstad in Northern Sámi areas (Myrvoll 2000: 52). *Ulda* is related to the Swedish word "hölja," meaning "to cover" (Kulonen 2005: 136). *Ulda* is the word used by Lule Sámi and Northern Sámi living at or close to the Swedish area (Kulonen 2005: 136, Holmberg 1915/1987: 76, Johan Turi 1910, 1920.) *Gufithar* comes from the Norwegian word "go-vetter," meaning good-spirit, and is to be found in Northern Sámi areas (Qvigstad, Johnsen 2005, Nergård 2006) and Inari/Utsjoki/Tana (Pentikäinen 1997: 232–234, Ravila, Itkonen). *Kadnihah* is the only word with Sámi etymology and of unknown meaning (Kulonen 2005: 206, Bäckman 1975: 131) according to Lars Levi Læstadius. It is reported as used by Sámi by Wiklund and Grundström (Bäckman 1975: 132).

I will employ the word *gufithar* because it is probably the most used term in Northern Sámi. These beings are described by some as key regulators of the relationship between humans and the local environments. They are treated as guardians of the places they are living at and impose a specific value system as to the use of local pieces of soil. *Gufithar* live under the ground in fixed places without sunshine. They are normally invisible but can appear and interact, even intermarry, with humans. They have a positive and a negative side. They are helpers and teachers but also a potentially disturbing, destructive force (Kulonen 2005: 87, Myrvoll 2010: 195). *Gufithar* play a key role in Sámi mythology. "The underground spirit offered advice, helped, gave warnings, protected and comforted" (Outakoski 1991: 160). They are seen as having taught them important skills, amongst others so-called magic and the traditional chanting, the "yoik." *Gufithar* are briefly mentioned in early missionary recordings (Skanke quoted in Mebius 2007: 89).

They have attracted quite some interest from theologians[80] and scholars.[81] Underground people are classical figures in recordings of oral stories and are generally described as a living religious tradition that is openly related to in the media.[82]

The underground people are a current theme in Sámi culture as well as in all Scandinavian mythologies and folk tales.[83] The stories about them have many common features that can be summarized as follows. *Gufithar* are more beautiful, richer and happier than humans. They wear Sámi clothing, speak the Sámi language, and are of small size. They live like humans and herd reindeer and keep cattle. They own much gold and silver. They help humans sometimes with the herding of reindeer or cattle, or they give them premonitory warnings about catastrophes such as bad weather or falling rocks.

There are many ways in which Sámi and *gufithar* interact. It is possible for a Sámi man to capture a *gufithar* woman and marry her. *Gufithar* can become jealous of beautiful human children and swap their children with Sámi children. A Sámi that finds himself lost can be captured by *gufithar* and might be forced to live with them forever, never to return to his human family.

Subterranean spirits are generally neither worshipped nor made offerings to (Bäckman 1975: 131, Johnsen 2005, Myrvoll 2010). Some authors though mention offerings of food and beverage. Turi (2011: 195) mentions a type of taxation, "vearro," to *uldda* as a reward for guarding reindeer. Southern Sámi underground spirits, *muenesje*s, have been told to request reindeer as an offering in the nineteenth and early twentieth centuries (Holmberg 1915/1987 76, Mebius 2007: 89–90).

Underground people can be overpowered with well-established rituals using objects of metal or with Christian symbols. Newborn children receive a silver ball in their cradle to prevent *gufithar* from bothering them. A *gufithar*

---

80 Here I will discuss the texts of the theologians Lars-Levi Læstadius, Niila Outakoski (1991) and Tore Johnsen (2005).

81 Some of the scholars that I use in this analysis are Holmberg (1915/1987), Bäckman (1975, 1991), Pentikäinen (1997), Mebius (2007) and Myrvoll (2000 and 2012).

82 An official Norwegian governmental report mentions that Sámi today believe in them (NOU 1998: 21 § 6.3.22): "Utredning om alternativ medisin."

83 All Qvigstad books have stories about them; see also Turi 1910.

has to give its herd to a Sámi when he manages to throw his knife over the *gufithar*'s herd. A *gufithar* girl has to marry a Sámi if he sticks her with a needle. Parents can put a Bible under the bed of a child that sleeps poorly because of an underground spirit's disturbance (Myrvoll 2000 writes about these customs related to children). They have greater power than humans when it comes to building houses. A wrongly placed house can be damaged or destroyed when a *gufithar* gets angry.[84]

Gufithar are supposed to be everywhere and always close by. They dislike lies, dishonesty, noise or any disturbance of the places where they live. All people, also children, have to be honest and subdued in order to preserve good reciprocal relations with the underground spirits. Underground spirits watch over their own dwellings and cattle and do not tolerate any human interlopers. If rules are transgressed then they can apply punishments such as damaging human dwellings, causing accidents or making cattle or people sick (Qvigstad passim).

They are generally seen as guardians of a value system and can protect or punish transgressors (Myrvoll 2010: 195, see quotation below). In recent sources, *gufithar* are often described as superhuman authorities of whom one must ask permission by using allowance-rituals before interfering with the soil. As a consequence of this, they have been described by some Sámi scholars, especially Johnsen and Myrvoll, as having a function in safeguarding local ecosystems:

> I believe that the belief in the huldra represents a view of nature management and environmental protection from which we can learn much today. When the landscape and the nature were "populated" by others, even if they were underground spirits and not humans, the relationship with the natural surroundings became characterized by equality. Humans had to treat nature as their neighbor and peer. Humans were at the same level and not superior to creation, and one adapted to the other. There was respect and certainty that one was in a relationship of reciprocity – in other words, a type of ecological sustainability (Myrvoll 1999: 29).[85]

---

84 When living in the Sámi area 2001–2009, I heard several of such stories.

85 "Jeg tror at troen på huldra representerer et syn på naturforvaltning og miljøvern som vi kan lære mye av i dag. Når landskapet og naturen var 'befolket' med andre, selv om de var underjordiske og slett ikke mennesker, ble forholdet til de naturskapte omgivelsene preget av likeverdighet. Mennesket måtte behandle naturen som sin nabo og likeverdige. Man var på likefot og ikke over det skapte, og man innordnet seg hverandre. Det bestød respekt og vissheten om at man sto

In these contemporary texts written in times of ecological crisis, the traditional role of underground beings as guardians over local ecosystems is seen in a new light. One wonders if the role of underground beings as important guardians for sustainable ecological values could be deepened and supported with concrete examples in future research.

Terminology and Scholarly Debates on Categories of Spirits

Even if their designation varies in different Sámi areas, underground people of the *gufithar/kadnihah/ulda* type are believed to be a coherent and stable group of superhuman agents distinct from other types of superhuman agents. Louise Bäckman wrote that the underground spirits were traditionally a separate category (Bäckman 1975: 130) but that religious change has melded the various classifications. "According to traditional material, the Sámi had earlier known a category of beings that corresponded entirely to the Scandinavian "underground people" (Bäckman 1975: 130).[86] In the contemporary anthropological study of Marit Myrvoll, this melding effect is unconfirmed. She states: "Stories about the underground spirits go back a long way and extend from the South Sámi area to the Kola Sámi in the northeast, from the coast to the inlands. The stories have many common features (Myrvoll 2010: 198).[87] The underground spirits are here treated as a separate type of superhuman agent with an independent existence and identity. This is also the situation I encountered in during my interviews. Underground people were linked neither to ancestors nor animal guides nor was their aid requested in hunting nor were they given offerings (SP, ST, anonymous person).

In the Northern, and Inari and Skolt area they are known as *háldi, guhfitarat, ulda* or *ganij* (sg), *gadniha* (pl) (Myrvoll 2010: 191). In Southern

---

i et gjensidighetsforhold, – med andre ord det som vi kaller i dag bærekraftig utvikling" (Myrvoll 1999: 29).

86 "Enligt tilgängligt traditionsmaterial har samerna tydligen känt en väsenskategori helt överensstämmande med skandinavernas 'underjordiska'" (Bäckman 1975: 130).

87 "Fortellingene om de underjordiske finnes i hele det samiske området, de strekker seg over et langt tidsspenn og kommer fra sørsamisk område til kolasamene i nordøst, fra kyst og innland. Fortellingene har mange fellestrekk fordi erfaringene med de underjordiske er stort sett de samme fra område til område" (Myrvoll 2010: 198).

Sámi they are called *saajve* (Mebius 2007) but questions still remain in this regard and further research is needed. *Saajve* are said to be related to the *sáivo* people that primarily represent ancestors and animal guiding spirits, who require sacrifices and live in a holy mountain. *Saajve* do not resemble the other underground spirits (Jernsletten 2004). In the Lule/Umeå region they are called *kanji* or *kemij* (Kulonen 2005: 92).

For Itkonen (1946: 70, 78–80, 104, 115) and Ravila (1934: 48, 54, 66, 71 and others) *háldi* designates ownership – or management of types of local spirits. Louise Bäckman also imputes other meanings to *háldi* (1975: 133); see the discussion in section 4.2. For Læstadius the Finnish concept of "halddo" is the same as *ganidha* and is closely related to the *sájva*. *Sájva* or *sáivo* are various types of important spirits that live in holy mountains and can travel from there to humans so as to accompany them (Bäckman 1975: 129). Nilla Outakosti believed that underground spirits are a replacement for the *sájvo* (Pentikäinen, 1997: 230). Bäckman wrote that underground spirits, as the ancient religion disappeared, collected the properties of various types of spiritual agents that were more independent in earlier times, like *háldi* and *sájvo* (1975: 129, 138). In general there were many different spiritual beings in nature and around the house and it can be difficult to identify separate categories; they might flow over into each other, states Mebius (2007: 92).

Theologians and the Underground Spirits as Personifying the Earth

Due to their strong presence in Sámi culture, the numerous beliefs and rituals associated with them, their attachment to the soil and the earth, and because they do not have a place in the Christian worldview, underground spirits have attracted much attention from Christian priests. The priests' attitudes toward them has substantially shifted over the last 150 years.

The charismatic Sámi priest Lars Levi Læstadius (1800–1866), founder of a well known religious movement named after him, spent some years actively combating the rituals and beliefs in underground spirits. He had dedicated seven of his 45 "Lappish sermons" to them in the period before 1853 (as enumerated by Outakoski 1991: 159) in which he demonizes the underground spirits. They came to be seen as an incarnation of evil and represented people who did not believe in Christ. It was their earthly connection and influence on the Sámi's daily life that was designated as "enemies to the cross," in complete opposition to the ideal of a kingdom of Christ that was to be in heaven (Outakoski 1991: 159, 160).

> How could they (the underground people, MB) come from earth to heaven if they cannot bear to hear about the cross which is a rightful sign of Christ? (...) They will never be released from the earth; they do not tolerate the light, because their acts are evil. (Læstadius 1988: 455 quoted in Myrvoll 2010: 206.)[88]

Læstadius recorded the orally transmitted myth of the origins of the underground people which connects them to the Old Testament. It presents them as a different type of human, as old as humans themselves.[89] For unknown reasons Læstadius lost interest in the underground spirits shortly after the dramatic Kautokeino uprising in 1852 and did not mention them any more in his sermons (Outakoski 1991: 159).

Nilla Outakoski (1909–2003) was a Finnish Sámi priest and Sámi cultural activist. He never served a parish in a Sámi area. After his retirement he obtained a doctorate in theology with his book about underground spirits in the work of Lars-Levi Læstadius, whom he calls his spiritual father (Outakoski 1991: 163).

Outakoski sees the underground spirits as replacement for the ancient Sámi gods and other aspects of ancient Sámi religion that came to be forbidden. He underscores the fact that Læstadius never denied their existence. To the contrary, he confirmed their reality. Outakoski is not judgmental toward the continuing belief of Sámi in these spirits, as they impose good values:

> The Christian symbols were placed underneath the Lappish gods, and the Lapps continued to hold the Christian faith secondary to their own religions. When the rumbling of the drums finally died down, a small pocket-sized underground spirit, easy to hide and endowed with the best Christian values and motives, replaced the troll-drum (Outakoski: 162, 163).

---

88 "Hvordan skulle de kunne komme fra jorden til himmelen når de slett ikke tåler å høre om dette kors som er en rett kristens kjennetegn.(...) De vil aldri slippe opp fra jorden, og de tåler heller ikke å se lyset, for deres gjerninger er onde" (Læstadius 1988: 455 quoted in Myrvoll 2010: 206).

89 The myth is as follows: The underground people were children of Adam and Eve. When God came to visit Eve, she had not cleaned all her children, and hid those that were dirty so he would not see them. Therefore God punished them by making them live forever underground. This story is not to be found in the Bible (Myrvoll 2000).

Tore Johnsen (b. 1969), Sámi priest of the Lutheran Norwegian state church from Tana/Finnmark, has occupied leading positions in the Sámi Church Council since 2007. He did fieldwork extending over several months with a group of reindeer herders in the Tana/Gamvik area in Eastern Finnmark. He has written about Sámi nature theology in recent years. He compares the underground spirits to Christian spirits such as angels (Johnsen 2005: 40) and does not condemn practices and stories associated with them.

> The underground people seem to traditionally have a key function in the relationship between humans and nature. They represent nature in a special way and can take action on behalf of nature. In their role as "guardians" or "rulers" of special places, they are key figures that impose frontiers and give direction to the impact of humans on nature. One might say that the stories about the underground people are to a high degree the expression of Sámi ecological knowledge, formulated in the language of the myth. (...) God has given the underground spirits a special task linked to nature. They represent the interest of nature toward humans and become a type of administrators of the *luonddu lágat*, laws of nature (Johnsen 2005: 65).[90]

Underground people are here described as personifying nature and representing sustainable ecological values. They are also seen as key agents in a religious worldview to maintain ecological values. Johnsen has an interpretation that strongly differs from the views of Læstadius and Outakoski. Outakoski had defended the idea that he beliefs and practices relating to underground spirits existed in parallel and independent of the Christian religion and even as a type of subversive "underground" Sámi identity-factor remaining from the pre-Christian belief system. Johnsens' own opinion is that this belief must find a place in the Christian Sámi nature theology that he is developing. This corresponds to the findings of Marit Myrvoll in a Læstadian Lule Sámi context. Sámi she dialogued with considered the Christian God to be the highest god who rules over everything, included the underground people.

---

90 „De underjordiske synes i tradisjonen å inneha en nøkkelfunksjon i relasjonen mellom mennesker og naturen. De representerer naturen på en spesiell måte og kan opptre på naturens vegne. I kraft av sin rolle som 'voktere' eller 'rådere' over bestemte steder, er de nøkkelfigurer som setter grenser for og gir retning til menneskets fremferd i naturen. Man kan si at fortellingene om de underjordiske i stor grad er uttrykk for den samiske økologiske kunnskapen, bare formulert i mytens språk. (...) Gud har gitt de underjordiske en spesiell oppgave knyttet til naturen. De representerer naturens interesser overfor menneskene og blir en slags forvaltere av luonddu lágat (naturens lover)" (Johnsen 2005: 65).

"The only thing we changed, was the upper row of gods"[91] stated one Sámi woman, referring to the levels of superhuman forces known from Sámi drums (Myrvoll 2010: 1, 7, 254–255). Læstadius is known to have respected and incorporated a number of elements of Sámi religious traditions, for instance in ecstasy, visions and shamanic journeys (Gjessing 1953 quoted in Zorgdrager 2000: 195–197). Even that thesis has been questioned, as Læstadianism can also just be seen as part of the wave of European revival movements that opposed itself to the godlessness of the French Revolution while at the same time expressing its autonomy of the individual and valorizing or even glorifying the (poor) common people (Minde 1998: 16).

Contemporary Beliefs and Rituals regarding Underground People and Ecology

It is from local storytelling traditions that the local people would know in which places underground spirits had been seen or were known to be living. In my experience, certain contemporary Sámi like to tell *gufithar* stories to their friends and neighbors. The only time humans address them actively is when they interfere with the soil. Then they have to ask for permission.

There are many examples of the permission-asking ritual before building. The procedure is as follows: The person who wishes to build a house must sleep one night in the place that is planned. The reply of the underground spirits will normally be given in a dream. A good night's sleep means a positive answer, a disturbed sleep or bad dreams must be seen as a refusal (Myrvoll 2010, also Nergård 2006: 155–158). Probably the traditional ritual could be much more elaborate, as the following example from the Sámi highschool building in Kautokeino shows.[92] Before the site of the building was finally decided, the rector of the Sámi high school herself initiated a ritual to consult the underground spirits. After the night's sleep in a tent on the proposed construction site, the spirits were interpreted to have given their permission to build. But one can question what the relevance for ecological sustainability was in this permission ritual. The building and the housing

---

91 „Det eneste vi har byttet ut, er øverste guderekke." (Myrvoll 2010: 1, 255).
92 News item: Doubting if ancient Sámi traditions were obyed to (Tviler på om gammel samisk skikk ble fulgt) NRK 26.10.2010. http://www.nrk.no/kanal/nrk_sapmi/1.7398832 read on 28.10.2015. See translation in the appendix.

sector have special attention in environmental policies so as to reduce their environmental impact. The high–school building that was planned and that has now been built has no special characteristics in terms of its environmental friendliness. It is not one of the ecologically exemplary building projects, like passiv-active or plus houses. Neither is it carbon-neutral nor has the Sámi high school been asked to be part of an ecological certification schema for institutions. The underground spirits obviously did not request that the rector make it into such a project.

Solveig Tangeraas explained that in her childhood in the 1950s she knew people who did not dig a hole or choose a fixed place to throw away dirty water without having asked the underground spirits. She told the story of a family that had built a new house. One day an underground spirit was seen walking along the fence, on the outside of it. This was interpreted as a sign that the underground spirit respected their appropriation of the place. Solveig also had personally spoken to a woman who had had two underground spirits as playmates during her youth. When she moved to a larger place, the two underground spirits came to visit her. They came only to say that they found it too noisy in town and that from then on they were not coming to play with her anymore (ST April 2013).

Some more stories about the role of underground people in connection with building dwellings and using grazing lands for reindeer-herding can be found in the book of Jens-Ivar Nergård (2006) about the Sámi traditional reindeer herding. Nergård has done fieldwork and conducted interviews with several reindeer-herders at various places in the Northern Sámi area. According to the author, traditional reindeer herders were not considered competent if they had not mastered the two aspects – the oral traditions and also the direct contact with the "soul of the area" or "the guardian of the place," personified by the appearance of various superhuman agents, amongst them underground spirits (Nergård 2006: 98–99, 105, 120–122). Contact with such superhuman agents are, according to Nergård, responsible for keeping a general balance within the limits of the local ecosystems of the reindeer-grazing lands (2006: 128). The general principles are clear and they sound interesting, but neither Nergård nor any other author elaborates or gives concrete examples of how these type of decisions affect the sustainability of grazing lands. Nowadays it is the state authorities that impose reindeer numbers and rights to use certain grazing lands. Is the ancient system still relevant, and how did it change after state regulation overpowered the traditional regulating mechanisms? How did or do the spirits keep the lands safe from overuse? The overgrazing by reindeer of large areas in Finnmark has been a highly debated subject on the public agenda for many years.[93]

One other anonymous informant explained to me that there were a couple of places near her childhood home where the underground spirits lived and how they would scare her away from spots where she had been forbidden to play as a child. One place was close to a cliff where stones could fall down, another place was close to a swamp where a child might be at risk of drowning. According to her, such stories of underground people were made up by the adults. She also told me about a spiritual experience she had when half asleep lying on the ground near her house in the summer. She suddenly saw tiny underground people dressed in shining clothes walking around on top of the soil. She had the thought that what the Sámi saw as underground spirits were in fact insects which people's imagination had transformed into *gufithar*. She concluded that the underground people were a creation of the human mind in order to fulfill an ecologically sustainable function – namely to show respect for the needs of certain insects that live on and under the earth. Familiarity and interactions with the spirit life around her house as she grew up gave her a deep sense of identity rooted in the area. Even if she realized that they were constructed by the human mind, including her own, this did not diminish her appreciation for the importance of the stories and her personal experiences. She could not imagine moving away from where she had grwn up. She felt a close familiarity with it through her life-long relationships to realms of the invisible world. This gave her a deeply felt sense of belonging.

These stories from the informants show two aspects – how much the living belief in interaction with underground spirits contributes to attachment and empathy with the local ecosystems, how important it is considered by this informant to protect even the smallest animal life, and how animals can be personified and idealized.

---

93 According to the report entitled «Riksrevisjonens undersøkelse av bærekraftig reindrift i Finnmark». (the Auditors Generals' Investigation on the Sustainability of Reindeer Herding in Finnmark) Document nr: 3:14 (2011–2012), 14.06. 2012, Sámi reindeer-herding in almost the entire province of Finnmark is not ecologically sustainable due to overgrazing and too many reindeer.

Conclusions as to Ecological Sustainability and the Underground People

Based on these findings, I wish to draw five conclusions as to the ecological sustainability of underground people.

First: Underground spirits are a form of local non-human personhood that represents a part of nature in particular ecosystems of the soil. This is illustrated in the insect story of one of my informants and in the considerations of past Christian clergy who reacted strongly to superhuman agency bound to the soil. Soil is itself an ecosystem that consists largely of living beings, many of them microscopic in size; fungi, protozoa, bacteria, small insects, etc. Seen as human persons, these create identification and empathy that induce humans to protect them.

Second: In the permission-seeking rituals associated with underground spirits they have been granted authority for deciding on the use of local eco-systems, an authority that is grounded in important sanctioning power. Some sources consider mastery of the stories to be a prerequisite for the establishment of sustainable relationships with local ecosystems. Underground spirits do not like noise or any unnecessary disturbance, and undisturbed nature is the place they thrive best, not in towns. That ritual has a significant preventive effect on human attitudes and behavior but does not seem to respond to modern ecological challenges. Underground spirtis give permission for building huge and ecologically unsustainable buildings and do not seem to oppose the overgrazing of reindeer pastures. Their role in imposing ecologically sustainable forms of life in contemporary Sámi culture can be said to be rather limited. As to the past, the information available does not allow any strong conclusions. It could be supposed that more concrete forms of effective ecological agency could be found when researching more detailed stories and doing more fieldwork with such as reindeer-herders.

Third: underground people have simultaneously an autonomous existence and a superhuman guiding/helping/teaching role. *Gufithar* have their own family and society life independent of humans. They are in some ways representative of an ideal – having superior powers and being very beautiful and happy.

Undisturbed local natural environments are seen as autonomous of humans and are idealized. Their role for guiding and teaching is not explained too frequently. It can be found in fiction, like in the novel of Kirstti Paltto (2012).

Fourth: Belief in underground spirits provides a feeling of safety and wholeness on the local scale. Where underground spirits live, it is a positive and safe place to be. The negative influences can normally be easily averted by adults. When respecting the rules they impose, one gets much in return: teaching, a safe house, warning of unexpected disasters, and a general sense of guidance and protection.

Fifth: They are providers of meaning and identity. The belief in underground spirits creates strong local identification; identification with the places that people know stories from, identification with close friends or relatives who have experienced them. Sámi scholars underscore that the belief in underground spirits is fundamental for a Sámi traditional identity (Outakoski 1991, Nergård 2006). Having met an underground spirit is seen as having special significance in the life of humans that encounter them. The experience includes that person or persons in a superior superhuman realm, which thereby gives confirmation of that person's life by acknowledging that it has value. They bind people to particular places where they have long-term relations with the local stories about the underground spirits.

6.2 *Sieidi*: Local Superhuman Agency and the Management of Resources

Sieidi and *háldi* are Northern Sámi names for superhuman authorities that manage the fauna and flora of a limited area. They have the central role of being the superhuman "official" intermediate or manager for local human communities with the natural resources over which they rule and which at the same time bind the hunters and fishers to obey a set of traditional hunting and fishing rules. *Sieidi* and *háldi* had to be addressed actively by ritual activity or other forms of religious attention. *Háldi* with a resource-management function can also be free-roving and mostly invisible spirits that belong to a natural area like the forest-*háldi* or the water-*háldi* (Itkonen 1946: 70, 78–80, 104, 115 and Ravila 1934: 48, 54, 66, 71).

Sieidis are present in all Sámi areas with similar functions. *Sieidi* can have the physical appearance of a stone, a part of a mountain, a tree, a carved pole of wood, or a spring (Kulonen 2005, Mebius 2007). Stone *sieidis* have the main focus in this chapter because they play a central role in Sámi religious life and there is more information on them.

Sieidis are considered a central feature in ancient Sámi religion (Mebius 2007: 145).[94] Most studies about Sámi religion have a chapter on *sieidis*. In descriptions of Sámi religion they are considered "shrines"– meaning objects that are worshipped and/or communicate with superhuman beings who have special powers (Kulonen 205: 389). One should be silent in the area around a *sieidi* and not hunt in the sacred area around the *sieidi*. Animals wounded by hunters that go to the sacred area around a *sieidi* should not be killed (Itkonen 1946: 13). Woman and dogs were not allowed to go near or even look at some *sieidi* (Holmberg 1915/1987: 33).

A *sieidi* might have various functions. There were local community *sieidis*. Every family once had once its own *sieidi* – at least this was said of the Uts-joki areas (Itkonen quotes Grape, Rheen and J. Fellman 1946: 12, Solbakk 2006: 34). Even an individual can have his own *sieidi* (Itkonen 1946: 12). In the olden days many *sieidis* were places for performing collective or in-dividual rituals and were linked to exclusive rights of use granted to a given area (Bäckman 1991: 21). In this analysis we will limit ourselves to their role in establishing and regulating relationships with the use of local natural ecosystems for harvesting resources.

Today's *sieidi* are often still objects of respect (Oskal 1995). They are places where people have spiritual experiences (Solbakk 2006, Jernsletten 2004 on the Southern Sámi area). "One can get on speaking terms with a *sieidi*, and even quarrel with it, and it can get very stubborn" – these are some recorded experiences of reindeer-herders from fieldwork done in the Northern Sámi area by Nils A. Oskal. A *sieidi* can help to get a large reindeer herd; but this is not a sustainable way of keeping reindeer because the reindeer luck will only hold for a single generation.

The worship of a *sieidi* is considered a sin, as it is seen as consisting of worship to gods other than the Christian one. Behaving respectfully toward

---

94 Link to a news item about Åke Solbakk and the *sieidi* that affords luck to Salmon fishermen: http://www.nrk.no/kanal/nrk_sapmi/ardna/1.8343810, downloaded 15 May 2013; and a film clip of Åke using his drum: www.nrk. no/video/historiker_aage_solbakk_pa_en_sjamangrav/66D7673F63A651B5/ (downloaded 15 May 2013).

a *sieidi* – like greeting it and wishing it well – are not considered a sin but normal and even necessary practice for maintaining a good relationship with the invisible parts of the landscape (Oskal 1995: 140).

Still today coins are sometimes to be found at certain *sieidis* (Sveen 2006) and the well known Sámi historian Åke Solbakk has given televised statements to the effect that he sacrifices to *sieidis*, but that his neighbors don't reply when he asks them if they also do that.

Terminology of *Sieidi*

There are other recorded names for *sieidis* in various areas (Itkonen 1946: 19). The word *sieidi* is probably etymologically related to the word "siida" meaning the traditional local Sámi community (Kulonen 2005: 389). The term is not mentioned in Skanke and Jens Kildal but in many other old missionary and priestly accounts (Mebius 2007: 145). Sacrificial stones in all Sámi areas, also the Southern Sámi area, are known as "sjielegierka," and on the Swedish side as "sjielevaajja" as described by J. Jernsletten (2004: 46) and Mebius (2007: 152–153) and on the Russian side on the Kola a *sieidi* can be called *ibmil* (god) or *Storjunckare* in Lule Lappmark (Rheen quoted in Bäckman 1991: 21).

Some *sieidis* are named after animal species by local oral tradition – for instance the otter-*sieidi* is known as "Čæwres-ibmel" (Vorren 1993: 122) or just fish-god, namely "Guolle-ibmel" (Vorren 1993: 115) and "Goose-stone" in Sorsele/Sweden (Manker 1965: 92).

Appearance of the *Sieidi*[95]

Sieidis are most frequently natural free-standing stones or parts of mountain formations that somehow have a special shape and are usually positioned significantly in the landscape. They can be huge, normal or rather small; be very visible on mountain and hilltops or on river or lake shores; close to or on the seashore and visible from the water at long distances and serving as a point of orientation; or they can be anywhere in the landscape (Vorren 1993: 131). They might have holes and crevices to deposit sacrifices (Vorren 1993: 29).

---

95 See Arvid Sveen 2003, Vorren 1993, Manker 1965, and Solbakk 2006 for books with numerous photos of recognized *sieidis*.

Stone *sieidis* regularly have anthropomorphic shapes like the profile of a human face (Pentikäinen 1997: 133). They can have the shape of a phallus or have holes like a vulva, be round-shaped like a human head, can be flat or upright. They can also be zoomorphic, resembling a bird for instance (Manker 1975). The *sieidi* stone or tree stump was used to place offerings on, under or next to them. The *sieidi* was often surrounded by a cultic area where collective rituals would take place. It might be surrounded by smaller stones, a fence of green twigs in the summer or antlers (Holmberg 1915/1987: 31). A *sieidi* could also be part of a larger sacred area (Mebius 2007: 139).

Scholarly Debate about the Nature of the Power of the *Sieidi*

In general *sieidis* are supposed to have a certain invisible power called "numinous" or "mana" (Kulonen 2005: 390). *Sieidis* are places "in which a god or spirit lives" says Itkonen, who feels that the god was not the stone itself but that the power of spirits was associated with the stone (1946: 12). According to the ancient missionary Torneaus, Sámi "called, loved, prayed to and worshipped *sieidis* like gods" (quoted in Mebius 2007: 146).

*Sieidi*s can but do not have to be associated with any particular named and personified god. We have testimony about a family's *sieidis* that represented *Dierpmes* or *Beaivi* in the Utsjoki area (J. Fellman quoted in Itkonen 1946: 12) or *Akka* in places like Sompio and Muddusjarvi (Itkonen 1946: 6, 7). One known *sieidi* is named after a god called Ibba: the Ibbakirku in Tana/Finnmark (Sveen 2006). A number of *sieidis* are related to the *Storjunckare* (Manker 1965: 96, 111). "There were *sieidis* that were not consecrated to a known divinity but only to the spirit of that particular place" (Itkonen 1946: 12).[96]

They also are sometimes described as becoming visible in the shape of a human or bird (Kulonen 2005: 391, Holmberg quoting Olsen and Fellman, 1915/1987: 35). Itkonen quotes a story of the destruction of an "akka" *sieidi* that turns first into a naked child and finally into a water bird (1946: 7). Some Swedish Sámi believe that a *sieidi* is a bird which came from the sky and then became stone (Holmberg 1915/1987: 36).

---

96 "Es gab *Sieidi*s, die keiner bekannten Gottheit, sondern nur dem Geist der betreffenden Stelle geweiht waren" (Itkonen 1946: 12).

There are several scientific theories on how to interpret the *sieidis*. For Uno Holmberg and Petterson, who wrote in the mid-nineteenth century, they are linked to ancestor worship and the spirits of the *sieidi* are various types of spirits linked to the clan or family (Kulonen 2005: 391, Bäckman 1991: 22). Hultkranz wrote in 1962 that they represented the underground spirits (quoted in Bäckman 1991: 20) or were simply the expression of an idea of the divine (Mebius in 1968, quoted in Bäckman 1991: 20).

With her focus on the separate identity of animal guardian spirits, Louise Bäckman summarizes the scholarly debate and concludes as follows:

> The *sieidi* marked the center of an area that belonged to the genius loci, under whose ægis was the flora and fauna of the territory. It was in this capacity that the genius acted as the Master of the Animal, *hallde* in Northern Saami. The territory was the hunting and fishing area of the *siida* group" (Bäckman 1991: 22).

That definition corresponds to the role of the *sieidi* as I have encountered it in my interviews and research in source for the last 100 years. The *sieidi* can reflect and represent all aspects that are of interest within a delimited landscape as to the hunting and fishing of humans. Its role is always related to the human need of fishing, it does not have any autonomous life of its own. Its absolute managing authority is part of the ancient system of the local community that has divided the access to hunting and fishing areas meticulously amongst families and communities, and when the ancient religion was still legal, and foreigners did not have the right of access to the hunt in that area (Bäckman 1991: 22).

The relationship between man and the *sieidi* was "relatively egalitarian and reciprocal" (Kulonen 2005: 390). According to Itkonen, a fisherman that starts using a lake that no one has used before first consecrates a stone and makes it into a *sieidi*, "the lord of the fish" (1946: 19). Or one could sleep a night next to it to find out if he received the message in a dream that it was suitable as *sieidi* (1946: 12). Holmberg quotes Rheen on how Sámi could decide to consecrate a new stone as *sieidi* (Holmberg 1915/1987: 37). The *sieidi* had the task of providing success in hunting and fishing, and the human should offer and respect the *sieidi*. It is part of the traditional belief system that the *sieidi* has power and it punishes those who do not respect it. But the humans could also punish the *sieidi* if it did not perform well by abandoning it or just arguing and getting angry with it. Oskal (1995: 140) tells of people arguing with *sieidi*.[97] "The people of the Teno River region are sometimes known to have beaten their fishing deities with birch switches to make them perform their duties better" (Kulonen 2005: 391). Humans could just turn them around or destroy them and consecrate new, more effective *sieidi*. Itkonen (1946: 57–58) and Fellman (quoted in Pentikäinen 1997: 139) have recorded stories about that.

Sanctions Show the Authority of the *Sieidi*

As to show how powerful a *sieidi* is supposed to be for animal populations, we can see what the sanctions are if they are removed or not respected. The stories recorded are similar in all Sámi areas and often concern fish. Removing a *sieidi* has dramatic negative consequences: the revenge always concerns humans, they lose their possibility of fishing. The animal perspective normally does not receive any empathic focus in the stories about removal or disrespect of *sieidis*. Animals are exclusively depicted in their role as resources for humans.

Apmut Kuoljok and John Kuoljok tell several stories about protests against the removal of *sieidis* in the Lule Sámi area by ethnographers some fifteen years ago. Von Rosen's expedition of 1900 visited several *sieidi*; some were in the shape of human heads, and most looked like dog heads (Kuoljok, Kuoljok & Westman 2010: 13). Assumed spiritual punishments in the form of sickness, reindeer death and wolf attacks occurred. Some local Sámi refuse to touch or lift up the *sieidis* and one that carried it got sick and dared not touch it anymore as a consequence. In 2003 a removed *sieidi* was placed in a ceremonial manner in the Sámi museum at the Ájtte museum in Jokkmokk situated in the area where it was taken from.

---

97 "One can get on speaking terms with a *sieidi*, and even quarrel with it, and it can get very stubborn," are some recorded experiences of reindeer-herders at personal fieldwork in the Northern Sámi area as related by Nils Oskal. A *sieidi* can help to get a large reindeer herd. But that is not a sustainable way to keep reindeer because the reindeer luck will only last for one generation. The worshipping of a *sieidi* is considered a sin, as it is seen to consist of worship of other gods than the Christian one. Behaving respectfully to a *sieidi*, like greeting it and wishing it good luck, is not considered a sin but normal and even necessary practice to keep a good relationship with the invisible parts of the landscape (Oskal 1995: 140).

There is also a story related by May-Lisbeth Myrhaug, without source reference, where an old and a younger man go fishing on a lake. The old man secretly sacrifices fish to the lake *sieidi*. The young man removes the *sieidi* and dumps it secretly at the bottom of the lake. The result is that they do not catch fish anymore. The old man notices the *sieidi* is gone, gets angry and the young man has to leave. The *sieidi* magically displaces itself to the old place, the old man sacrifices again, and he catches fish in huge amounts (Myrhaug 1997: 21–22).

A frequently recurring story is that removal of a *sieidi* causes the harvestable animal population to disappear or at least to be harmed. Jorum Jernsletten refers to this happening in the southern Sámi area (2004: 55).

There used to be a large white stone that was a seamark for fishermen to find their fishing grounds and a *sieidi* on a mountain ridge at the edge of the Porsanger Fjord in Finnmark/Norway. It was removed in the 1970s because the municipal assembly decided that it wanted to use it as a memorial stone for fallen soldiers. Local fishermen protested before and after the removal, using the argument that it was their mark. The removal was followed by an emptying of the fjord of seafish in the following years. According to S. Persen, this was caused by industrial trawler-fishing by people outside the fjord. The local communities have no direct power to stop trawlers from overfishing the fjord. Sigvald Persen tells how local fishermen saw the removal of the sacred stone as being in clear relation to the emptying of the fjord of fish.

A *sieidi* on the shore of a fish-rich inland lake in the Galanittu area near Kautokeino in Finnmark/Norway was removed by Norwegians with the aim of exhibiting it in Trondheim at the beginning of the twentieth century. Its removal was linked to the successive disappearance of fish from that lake. Persons from the Sámi community linked to the Sámi high school asked to get the *sieidi* back, and this was agreed upon. They placed it back around the year 2005 at what was believed to have been its original site. But the fish stocks did not return to the levels of 2008 when I had studied in Kautokeino and asked local people about the fish in the lake and the stone. Some said the *sieidi* was probably not placed at exactly the right place, and that this was the reason for the fish not returning (personal research in Kautokeino, autumn 2008).

Less dramatic than such removals is a punishment inflicted by the *sieidi*. One has to offer in the correct way, otherwise the *sieidi* becomes offended and punishment follows in the form of a bad catch (Dermant Hatt 1928 quoted in Jernsletten 2004: 55).

Sacrifice and Sustainability: Celebrating Community, Regenerating Life, Reciprocity and Respect for Behavioral Rules

In ancient times the ritual most often described as being part of the religious function of a *sieidi* is sacrificing. As described by ancient missionaries, it was frequent in Sámi sacrifical practice to cook a common meal of the sacrificed meats (Mebius 2007: 134–137). Sacrificing and the common meal were a kind of double communion – a communion between members of that local community which enjoys the right to use the *sieidi*, and with the superhuman power of the *sieidi* (Mebius 2007: 154 ff). An ecological aspect of sacrificing was that sacrifice of substances like grease or blood was also seen as a guarantee for that the population that the sacrificed animal would not be weakened. "The Sámi sacrifical tree was smeared in with blood, and that can be interpreted as an expression of a similar thought that is integral to the conservation of the bones of the hunted prey that the sacrifical animal regenerates" (Mebius 2007: 145).[98]

Sacrifices could be animal fat, blood, antlers and meat. Fish oil and fish heads (Kulonen 2005: 390) are mentioned as offerings to fish *sieidis*. But also metal objects, alcoholic drinks, and tobacco (Kulonen 2005: 390). If the sacrifice is right then the fishing, hunting or reindeer-herding will go well. The more sacrifices the better (Itkonen 1946: 13). Some missionaries have related cases of adults and children that were sacrificed (Itkonen quotes Tuderius, Olsen, Qvigstad and Varonen as sources 1946: 11, Holmberg quoting Olsen and Tuderus: 40) and according to some sources animals were even sometimes sacrificed alive, for instance by burying them under the ground or locking them up in a crevice of rock (Itkonen 1946: 15, Holmberg 1915/1987, 40). According to Laila Spik, whom I asked to comment on this records, to make an animal suffer in this way was against the Sámi value system, and she could not imagine that these practices had been common (LS August 2012).

---

98 "Då de samiska offerträna smörjes med offerdjurets blod kan detta uppfattas som ett uttrykk för en liknande tanke som hör samman med bevarandet av såväl jaktbytets som offerrenens skelettdelar, d.v.s. att offerdjuret regenereres" (Mebius 2007: 145).

The *sieidi* is actively involved in imposing a value system and rules for the use of the resources, with the aim of an ecologically sustainable use of it. The *sieidi* was a very strict god that demanded worshipping according to precise rules, states Itkonen (1945: 50). It was a basic value not to deplete the animal populations and to respect the lives and well-being of animals that the local communities[99] depended upon for immediate survival. In return, the spiritual authority of the resource "agrees" that humans are allowed to take out what they need. These values ensure that humans contribute to the maintenance and even creation of the best possible conditions for animals to reproduce and thrive. It is in this way that human access to resources remains secured.

Sámi sources make very clear the functions of the *sieidi* as an authority for imposing rules for sustainable harvesting. According to Elina Helander, an expert in local use of the Tana River area, the Sámi used to communicate with the fish through the *sieidi*: "Sámi spiritually communicated with the fish. Amongst others they did that via the many Deanu fish-*sieidis*. In that way they knew how much they could take and what to do and not to do so as to protect the fish that they knew they were dependent on" (Helander 2010: 5).

Sigvald Persen is also very well aware of this function of the *sieidi*: "Together with respecting the *sieidi*, one respected the value system that was attached to the traditional culture, for instance never fishing more than needed" (SP February 2013).

This reciprocity provides security. A contemporary Swedish Sámi confirms that *sieidi* has the function of providing security and confidence in nature.[100]

---

99 Every Sámi informant (SP, ST, LS) said that in the old days, local resources like caught fish or hunted animals were shared with members of the local community who had for whatever reason no chance of gathering that type of food themselves.

100 "The powers (...) that could influence the well-being and the dwellings, reindeer luck, the generosity of nature as well as the weather during daily work. But then came the new religion that did not accept the habits and costumes that our ancestors lived with. The sieidi should no longer be the visible transmittor of practices that purchased power and confidence from the surrounding nature" (Apmit Ivar Kuoljok, in Kuoljok Kuoljok & Westman 2010: 4). Swedish original: "De makter-... som kunne påvirke tilvaron och boendet, renlykan och naturens givmildhet samt påverka vädret infor det daglige arbeidet. Men så kom den nye religionen som inte accepterande de seder och bruk som våra

From these sources one can understand that respect for a *sieidi* as expressed in various rituals like sacrifice, communication or just greeting and paying your respects is a signal that the humans obey the traditional values of respect to the local ecosystems. "An individual can very well have understood sacrifice as an operation that requests a divine quid pro pro" (Mebius 2007: 157).[101] The superhuman ruling powers were trusted to respect their side of the reciprocity equation by providing good harvesting and using conditions.

The *Sieidi* as Guarantee of Ecological Sustainability

Scholars have frequently interpreted the *sieidi* as purely economical: "As a matter of fact, a *sieide* was worshipped for financial reasons; for luck in hunting and fishing and for good luck in reindeer-raising" (Bäckman 1991: 21). Manker talks about sacrifice "with very explicit utilitarian motives" (Manker quoted in Mebius 2007: 159).[102] In my view the utilitarian value is just one aspect of a larger complex of ecological relationships between the *sieidi* as superhuman agent representing the local resources and a given human group like a family or a community that has exclusive user rights for the area the *sieidi* is responsible for. I have distinguished three ways the *sieidi* plays a role in maintaining local ecological sustainability.

First, the local area-related *sieidi* becomes a managing authority over fauna and flora in specific surroundings like a lake, hunting area or reindeer-grazing land, e.g. for humans who wish to use the resources. It is given that superhuman negotiating authority by humans themselves, who in several areas are known to have consecrated the *sieidi* themselves.

Second, the *sieidis* have a collective role in enforcing community and collective sustainable management. Respecting a *sieidi* is a collective identity-confirming activity for the user group.

---

förfäder levt med. Sejten skulle inte längre vare den synbare förmedlaren av seder som hämtade kraft och tillit av den omgivande naturen" (Apmit Ivar Kuoljok in Kuoljok, Kuoljok & Westman 2010: 4).

101 "En enskild individ kan mycket väl ha uppfattat offret som en prestation som kräver en gudomlig motprestasjon" (Mebius 2007: 157).

102 "Offerhandlinger med rätt krassa nyttomotiv" (Manker quoted in Mebius 2007: 159).

Third, safety and survival by common agreement on reciprocity and implying mutual rights and duties. The basic assumptions behind this logic of reciprocity is that humans, animals and plants are part of a larger system where everybody has the right to thrive and mutual needs must be met. Humans have a right to catch animals so as to feed themselves, and animals have the right to live and thrive even if hunted. When the offering is made, respect is being shown and it is assumed that the humans follow the rules of good behavior, and a part of the sieidi's duty is to provide fish and game to the humans.

With the double aim of imposing the sustainable harvesting of animal resources even on the community level and securing the availability of nature resources, the *sieidi* was a powerful instrument for the ecological sustainability of local ecosystems that is necessary for the long-term survival of local Sámi communities in ancient times. The supernatural agency is even seen as indispensable to the survival of the hunted animal populations, as the removal of a *sieidi* causes the disappearance of the animals.

As for the historical development and limitation of the *sieidi* system, it is easy to understand that its role in imposing ecological sustainability depends on exclusive rights of use by a certain group in the long term. The functioning and authority of the *sieidi* is not intact if humans that are not familiar with the *sieidi* and the associated behavioral rules hunt or fish in the area it rules.

The aspect of the *sieidi* system which I found most interesting is that humans impose on themselves the superhuman authority by actively consecrating the *sieidis*. In a way they are aware of respect of ecological requirements are necessary to keep an animal population stable, and they seem to choose a supernatural agent as a type of "help" to enforce these rules.

6.3 Landscapes

The term "landscape" is holographic: it can designate a large undefined area but also a seemingly endless number of fragments that each form their own composite unit of various sizes, like a mountain, a lake, a river, a well, a forest or a larger area of grazing lands. In this text I wish to discuss two aspects of landscapes: landscapes that are seen as sacred and the perception of landscapes that do not have to be sacred but are considered to have status as a subject, having agency. In northern Sámi the term for landscape

116

is "eanadat," related to the words *eana,* meaning earth, and *eadni,* meaning mother; in southern Sámi "eatnama" means "my mother" (Jernsletten 2004: 54). But the terms used by sources vary, as the focus lies mostly lies on specific types of landscape.

Sacred Landscapes

In the Sámi tradition there are many sacred landscapes. The best known are the sacred mountains, called *basse-várri, saivo* or *áilegas,* and the sacred lakes called *sájvo.*[103]

Reindeerherder Ola Omma (b. 1923) spoke about the sacred Sálašoaivi Mountain near Tromsø and how their tradition dictated that one had to behave properly in the vicinity of this sacred mountain. Forbidden is any disturbance in the form of noise, loud talking or singing, or absconding with objects. They had to greet the mountain when passing by, their reindeer had to graze there three days every year, and one should not go to the higher parts of the mountain. The Sámi felt that they received healing and guidance from the mountain.[104]

Some of the ancient missionaries noted that every Sámi had one or several holy mountains where his or her ancestors and healing spirits were living and to whom the Sámi were sacrificing (Rydving 1995: 71–72). Skanke has noted the names and numbers of sacred *saivo* mountains "from Eastern Finnmark to Trondheim" (Rydving 1995: 187–189). As for the explanation as to why they are considered sacred – they are seen as a place where spirits like the

---

103 Some overviews: Qvigstad 1926, Lappische Opfersteine und heilige Berge in Norwegen; Manker 1957, Lapparnas heliga ställen; and Ørnulv Vørren 1993, Samiske offerplasser i Varanger. See also the recent master's thesis in archeology of Jon Gunnar Blom, 2011, on ethnicity and sacred sites, with an overview and maps of sacred Sámi sites, at the University of Tromsø. For pictures and stories, see also the online-exhibition of the Varanger Sámi Museum at www. saivu.com, in both Norwegian and English.

104 See bok 'Tinden' written and published by Arvid Sveen 2006, and news item of the Norwegian broadcasting company on 3.2.2003 about the Ola Omma, then 81. year old reindeer herder from Jokkmokk, who tells about living religious practices related to that mountain. http://www.nrk.no/nyheter/distrikt/ nrk_troms_og_finnmark/troms/3485920.html read on 29.10.2015...

sájvo people live and support humans in all aspects of their lives (Bäckman 1975).

Sacred landscapes are not directly and explicitly related to hunting and fishing success and the management of resources, even if the perception of them as sacred constantly reconfirms and recreates the traditional value system. The sacred landscapes have become part of contemporary debates on ecological protection, when Sámi wished sacred landscapes to remain untouched by planned commercial exploitation. Examples are the controversial public debates (Kraft 2004) over the pretended sacredness of Sálašoaivi Mountain, in Norwegian called Tromsdaltind, which the authorities planned to use as site for the Winter Olympic Games of 2018,[105] or the sacred spring Suttesája in the Utsjoki municipality of Finland. The Sámi parliament wrote a report that the mountain was holy and this was largely based on the testimony of a single person, none daring to question this person, and she adds that Norwegian law does not protect Sámi traditional beliefs, or, as she terms it, "nature religion," only the Sámi cultural heritage has has been proven to be over one hundred years old (Kraft 2004: 241). Suttesája is the largest natural spring in Finland. The municipality wished to allow its use for a company that wanted to bottle and sell the water on the commercial market. The plan raised a local cultural Sámi protest movement that had international repercussions.[106]

Landscape as Subject

Sámi scholar Nils A. Oskal (1995: 123) as well as Jorunn Jernsletten (2004) and Helander (2010: 45) have elaborated the subject or personhood status of landscape. Nils A. Oskal wrote his doctoral thesis on reindeer-herding luck,

---

105 Shortly after the information from Omma became public, the local Olympic planning commitee dropped the plans to use Sálašoaivi and decided to search for another potential location. Norway later withdrew its application for Tromsø as location for the 2018 Winter Olympic Games because the budgeted costs were estimated as too high (Kraft 2004: 238).

106 On Suttesája, see the chapter entitled "Suttesája" in Rauna Kuokkanen's Echoes From The Poisoned Well: Global Memories of Environmental Injustice, edited by Sylvia Hood (2006), Washington; and for the action of the international group Survival International in 2010, see http://www.culturalsurvival.org/publications/cultural-survival-quarterly/finland/water-prospecting-threatenssami-sacred-site; downloaded 16 May 2013.

which was based on long immersion in the world of the reindeer herders in Finnmark. He describes how reindeer herders must possess the capacity to communicate with reindeer-grazing areas due to the presence of various types of spirits such as *háldi, ulda,* underground beings, or *máddo* who are present in these places (Oskal 1995: 96). Tore Johnsen noticed that reindeer herders pray to both, the Christian gods and the various types of spirits that live in an area (Johnsen 2005: 28, 30, 39, Nergård 2006: 105, 121–122). To describe the landscape, Oskal and Johnsen use various terms like "reindeer-grazing lands," "summer/winter/autumn dwelling lands," "surroundings" and others (Johnsen 2005: 28, Oskal 1995: 103).[107] Landscape is generally treated as a coherent subject in itself that the herder must deal with in order to get along with it. That is an important part of the ethics of the reindeer-luck.[108] The rationalized reindeer herding that only obeys to rules imposed from the Norwegian authorities and modern market forces does not take into account the traditional values of honesty, fairness and respectfulness toward one's surroundings, including humans, reindeer and the land. For Oskal, those are the key ethical attitudes in traditional reindeer herding. On behalf of the aim of a more effective exploitation of grazing lands, it demands that the Sámi shake off their "reciprocal links and obligation to agree"[109] with the reindeer-grazing lands. The value of justice and the well-being of reindeer is for Oskal secondary to such purely commercial motives (Oskal 1995: 168).

Jorunn Jernsletten states that the Sámi have seen the landscape as an acting subject (Jernsletten 2004: 49) and mentioned not only the relations with a number of types of superhuman beings that live there and have historical and physical links to places but for instance the way that Sámi interpret their relationship to a forest as "mother and father," i.e. with reciprocity and mutual dependency (2004: 54, 56). The aim is to achieve a balance. This is expressed

---

107 Nils A. Oskal calls the various landscapes "birras," meaning surroundings, "reinbeiteland", in Sámi "guohtuneatnamiid"; the seasonal grazing lands are called "orohaga" (Oskal 1995: 103); and Tore Johnsen says the reindeer-grazing land is called "duovdda"(2005: 40).

108 "Soabadeapmi ii leat dušše mu duohken, muhto maid min ja mu birrasa duohken obanasiige. Mu soabadeapmi earaiguin sistisdoalla maid ahte earat leat soabadan muinna, ja ii ge nu go bággamis, gos mu bággan earaid ja earat leat bággaeallan munnje" (Oskal 1995: 123).

109 "Gjensidige bånd og samrådingforpliktelse" (Oskal 1995: 168).

in the Southern Sámi symbol of the "mirror image," an ancient decoration motif that bespeaks how the inner state reflects the outer.[110]

Landscape Rituals

These various types of rituals with the landscape as subject were not mentioned by ancient missionaries but are only known through more recent accounts. Emilie Demant Hetta recorded the acts of an old reindeer herder who, when he knew that his death was approaching, said farewell to the grazing lands as he journeyed through them one last time and cooked coffee that he poured on the soil as offering and asked for that the lands might feed those to come after him in the same way as they fed him (Demant Hetta 1928, quoted in Jernsletten 2004). We do not know if this was a common ritual or not. But from this quote it is clear that the value system aimed at long-term sustainable use by Sámi and resisted deterioration of the productive power of the ecosystems.

Oskal, Johnsen and Nergård refer to the rituals of permission-asking *lobiid jearrat* (Oskal 1995: 103). Another ritual called for the asking of blessings and thereby creating good luck, which is designated *sivnidit*.

Sámi also used to make crosses over reindeer land to bless it (Johnsen 2005: 29). The utilization and meaning of the symbol of the cross used by Sámi is described by Holmberg – for instance its use on the sacrificial world pillar of the upper god, on the wall of the hut at Christmas, and on the sacrificial bark boats hung on trees for the Christmas people. It is interpreted as the pre-Christian sign for a hammer, linked to the Sámi god *Horagallis*, which corresponds in many respects to the Norse *Thor* (Holmberg 1915/1987: 24, 25, 60, 114, Rydving 1995: 125). Amongst other meanings the cross is a symbol for the four cardinal directions. The Sámi were also aware of the four directions, as already described by Skanke (Rydving 1995: 127). He explains that the sun is depicted as a square on drums because it sends its power in all four directions. There is also the traditional Northern Sámi male "'four-winds hat," a hat often worn by men that consists of four pointed corners. For Tore Johnsen's informants the term *sivnidit* is different from those of Oskal

---

110   This symbol has been researched and described by Maja Dunfjeld (2001) in Tjaalehtjimmie: form og innhold i sørsamisk ornamentikk.

because for them it is exclusively related to addressing Christian forces. The well-wishing and thanking formulation to the grazing lands is something else. One important wish is that the grazing lands not be destroyed (Johnsen 2005: 29). One other ritual is the asking for peace, "vitkat." This was mostly done by a priest, according to Johnsen (2005: 26–27) and reflects the intention of establishing balance on a superhuman level with the landscape.

Communication with grazing lands via thoughts is mentioned (Johnsen 2005: 25). Thanking thoughts and prayers to the grazing lands and for the "gifts of God," *Ibmila láhjit*, after eating when diposing of bones were also a regular feature (Johnsen 2005: 20, 27–29, 62–63).

Ecological Sustainability and Landscape Agency

The subject perspective and the perception of the relationship of dependency on landscapes creates identification and empathy. Clearly expressed is a value system that promotes ecologically sustainable use. Unfortunately we do not have any concrete examples of what this perspective and the associated rituals have meant in the past or mean today in terms of concrete ways to achieve ecological sustainability. Does the grazing land sometimes say no to the entrance of a reindeer herd, and why? What kind of ecological reason could be found for that? The strong underlying value system might suppose such mechanisms. Meanwhile there is not one recorded story about a landscape forbidding the use of helicopters or motorized vehicles, which is common practice in today's reindeer herding. Here too it would seem that the traditional permission rituals do not prohibit the use of modern technology in our globalized society. Its concretization or any form of actualization is not being discussed beyond Oskal's bitter conclusion that the modern economic system is incompatible with his interpretation of Sámi reindeer herding ethics.

Chapter 7 – Global Agency

7.1 Nature: *Gullat luonddu jienaid*

As I read Tore Johnsen's study *Sámi Luondduteologiija* (*Sámi Nature Theology* I became aware of the fact that nature as a whole can become an actor in belief and ritual. My interest in this issue grew even stronger when I heard a young Sámi yoik singer criticizing mining activities in the Sámi reindeer area in Kvænangen in northern Norway. According to her, the Sámi had to ask themselves how to search for spiritual harmony with nature. She used the term "spiritual oneness with nature" – in Sámi: *vuoiŋŋalaš oktavuoda lundui* – to describe this issue. I started wondering what she meant by that term and whether it was commonly used.[111]

The statement that the Sámi consider themselves a part of nature and not separate from it, is often expressed as a way to oppose themselves to what is perceived as the "Western" separation between man and nature. It is the standard way academics with a Sámi perspective articulate their view of nature.[112] During my interviews I witnessed a discussion between two Sámi on this theme. It was on the occasion of a handicraft gathering in the Porsanger area (fieldwork in Nov. 2012). There were about ten ladies of various ages who knitted and sewed and Norwegian was the language used. After a while, one started to speak a little bit of Sámi. It turned out that most of them were native Sámi speakers. I was given the opportunity of explaining what my study was about and that I was curious as to their reactions and comments. One elderly lady who was not from a Sámi cultural background and did not speak Sámi immediately took the floor after I had spoken. She spoke with a loud voice and said: "God has given us fish and animals and all in nature, so we can take what we need." The Sámi did not say a word. In the car driving home, I asked Sigvald and another woman with us what they thought about what she had said. The woman replied that she disagreed because it sounded as if the humans were above nature and not a part of it.

---

111 I did not ask her directly because I did not plan to use her as informant, did not know her very well and did not wish to improvise and just drop a question in her lap about an important spiritual issue.

112 See chapter 3 for discussion and references.

So what is nature for Sámi and what terms do they use? I have recorded contradictory information about the meaning of the Northern Sámi word *luondu*.[113] According to some Sámi academics connected to the environment of the Sámi high school the term *luondu* – as the modern translation for "nature" and the same word used in Finnish, Norwegian, Swedish and English – is of recent origin and taken directly from the Finnish. For them *luondu* originally meant "characteristic" or "basic trait" in the Sámi language – as in the English phrase: "this horse has a friendly nature." The Sámi did not have any concept for nature as being separate from or non-influenced by humans, according to Magga (2011) in reference to linguistic research of the Sámi high school (as does Schanche 2002: 162). Nils A. Oskal for instance never uses the term *luondu* to describe surroundings. He uses the word to describe the ethics of the reindeer herders resulting in reindeer luck: "That does not mean that reasonability, honesty and irreproachability are natural, meaning that they are naturally present but that they should become part of human nature"[114] (Oskal 1995: 103).

This view was also confirmed by my interviews in Porsanger. Sigvald Persen and Solveig Tangeraas seemed almost irritated by what they perceived as a recent change in meaning of the ancient word *luondu* as designating the environment in the modern sense of the word. They believe this understanding has come about under the influence of the ecological movement, which they criticize for having had a negative impact on the Sámi traditional lifestyle and economic activity (Magga 2011, informants Persen and Tangeraas).

They also confirmed what the Sámi high school academics say, namely that in nature humans are never separate and therefore there is no Sámi term corresponding to the concept of untouched nature." *Meahcci* and *luohtu* express different places in the wilderness. *Meahcci* was the area around the place one lived and where humans obtained resources like fish, berries and wood. *Luohti* was further away and designated where one sent domesticated

---

113 *Luondu* is the nominative case, *luonddu* is the accusative/genitive case, *luondui* the illative case.

114 "Dat ii mearkkaš ahte rehalašvuohta, vuoiggalašvuohta ja gutnalašvuohta lea luonddolaš, dan ipmardusa mielde ahte dat boahtá luonddus, muhto baicce ahte dat galgašii <u>šaddat</u> olbmo luonduin" (Oskal 1995: 103).

animals to graze in the summer (Magga 2011). The same interpretation of these two words was also confirmed by Sigvald Persen and Solveig Tangeraas. Nevertheless *luondu* was confirmed by other persons as a general overarching word for nature seen as a whole on the global level. For Elina Helander-Renvall (2010: 45) the term is ambiguous, and "natural environment" was also part of its meaning. Laila Spik clearly confirmed the same. In her upbringing the word *luondu* had two meanings, the essence of something or someone and – its more normal usage – animals or humans or the natural environment seen as a whole. It was also for her a central concept for a set of important beliefs and rituals (LS May 2013).

Magga (2011) writes that "nature" is sacred to the Sámi. Here he can only mean nature as a whole. Jernsletten's Southern Sámi stated that the whole of nature[115] is sacred to them (Jernsletten 2002: 9). In modern Sámi Christian theology it seems that the word *luondu* has become the key term for a form of religiosity that can be related to the ancient religion.

The reindeer herders serving as informants for Tore Johnsen use the term *luondu* and "religion of nature" (*luondduosko*) for referring to beliefs and practices that are related to non-Christian superhuman agency in nature. *Luondduosko* emerges as a key term used by theologians to describe elements of ancient Sámi traditions that can be linked to the ancient religion (Johnsen 2005: 33). It is seen by many of his informants as the opposite of Christianity, something they worship in parallel to Christian gods.

> You really like nature very much and think about it, but should also in addition … remember at the same time God the Father and pray also to him. That is not a contradiction, really not. You shall do both. (…) And nature does of course not like that you believe more in God, the creator (…) Of course you can believe more in him, but the other part is anyhow like nature; the wilderness areas and everything that has been created there. One considers that God the Father has created that also. In this way you should (…) not reject it; neither one nor the other. That is also a part of what I learned from childhood on (Johnsen 2005: 41)[116]

---

115 "Hele naturen" (Jernsletten 2002: 9).
116 Du er veldig glad i naturen og tenker på den, men man skulle i tillegg…, men så husker man samtidig på Gud Fader og å be til ham også. Det står ikke i motsetning, slett ikke. Du skal begge.(…) Og naturen liker det selvfølgelig ikke dersom du tror mer på Gud, på Skaperen (…) … Du kan selvfølgelig tro

When keeping in mind that the informants are aware of talking to the leading priest of their local congregation, it might be possible that the belief in nature could be not be placed in too great opposition to belief in the Christian God. Johnsen underscores in his comments that the reindeer herders consider nature to be created by God and that the difference between God and nature is therefore not too important.

Johnsen quotes a series of terms that are related to *luondu*. All living beings are "creatures of nature," the *luonddugapaldagat*, and have to obey "natural laws," *luonddu lágat* in order to survive. To achieve survival one has to "listen to the voices of nature," *luonddu jienaid guldalit* (Johnsen 2005: 32, 34–35). The voices of nature ask for respectful attitudes and behaviors. When its directions are transgressed, nature can punish you (Johnsen 2005: 33).

Also Tore Johnsen concludes that nature is sacralized and placed at the same level as God. He then discusses how these beliefs can be framed within the Christian religion that he represents. Spiritual beings such as underground spirits and others are being summarized as "powers" that dwell in nature and he compares them to Christian angels (Johnsen 2005: 40, 49, 62, 65–67). The involvement with these is seen as popular belief (Johnsen 2005: 64, 65). Johnsen concludes that the Sámi traditional way of thinking corresponds very well to Christian motifs from the Bible. Humans are seen as stewards of nature who must respect all living beings (Johnsen 2005: 53, 57). Johnsen also underscores the importance of making an agreement with nature within the logic of concluding a pact. The term *luonddu láhjit* corresponds to thanking God for bestowal of his grace (Johnsen 2005: 39, 48, 62, 63). The book of Tore Johnsen ends with the affirmative statement: "We have nature Christianity" to describe Sámi religious identity (Johnsen 2005: 73) and he underscores the fact that the demonization of "earth worship"[117] has removed people from the landscape and erased a cosmological understanding of the world (2005: 34).

---

mer på ham, men den andre delen er likevel med, naturen; utmarka og alt som er skapt der. Man regner jo med at Gud Fader har skapt det også. Slik at du skal… og ikke forkaste det; verken det ene eller det andre. Det er også en del av det jeg har lært fra barndommen av" (Johnsen 2005: 41).

117   "Jorddyrkelse" is the word he uses (Johnsen 2005: 32).

Oktavuohta luondui – Oneness with Nature

I decided to investigate the concept *oktavuohta luondui* in greater detail so as to discover possible links to beliefs and rituals. As I interviewed informants on their ideas about *oktavuohta luondui*, I got varied replies.

For Tore Bongo, known as a Sámi politican and ancient Alta activist from the 1980s and now a Sámi school teacher, the concept was alive and well and acted as a type of inner guiding principle. I interviewed him in Alta in April 2013 and asked him only questions about this single concept. The reason for this was that he had recently been invited to speak before a gathering of young Sámi on Sámi values in Alta. I wished to know if that term had been a main issue in the debate. That had not been the case, he said. It was comparable to the allowance-asking ritual. *Luondu* was personified. He declared that he is able to feel when he is in harmony with nature and when not. "It sits in here," he stated and pointed to his heart. He just senses he is in unity with nature and when not. He is not in unity with nature when he is in an airplane or driving a motorized vehicle.

When I asked further, his spontaneous explanation was that noise disturbs nature.

Tore also linked the term *oktavuohta luondui* to the modern ecological challenges of today. For him the traditional Sámi expression for listening to the voices of nature was *gullát luonddu jienaid* rather than *oktavuohta luondui*. Tore stated that he grew up with this concept in the Sámi coastal village of Lahari, now a neighborhood of Alta, the largest city in Finnmark. He said that most Sámi people today have forgotten this guiding principle for concrete action. For him this concept was part of the basic values of traditional Sámi culture and had too small a role in the movement to strengthen Sámi values, in which he has been involved.[118] He said that he was one of the few Sámi who took it up at recent meetings with younger Sámi. Sigvald

---

118 The ČSV/Čájet Sámi Vuoiŋŋa movement, meaning "Show Sámi Spirit." Started in 1972 by preacher Anders Guttormsen at a gathering in Sirma, Finnmark, this was a very influential informal movement. The name 'ČSV' became for many years a central symbol of Sámi identity and self-assurance. http://sapmi.uit.no/sapmi/ExhibitionContainer.do?type=tema, from the "Sápmi Becoming a Nation" trilingual online exhibition staged by Tromsø University Museum; downloaded on 18 May 2013.

Persen and Solveig Tangeraas found that these words did not correspond to experiences from their upbringing. Another traditional young reindeer-herding Sámi I spoke to told me that she had heard it only as an adult and not as a child. She knew it as a concept from poetry and art. Tore Johnsen mentions that for some of his informants the concept of listening to the voices of nature[119] was a guiding principle for their behavior in nature, while others had not heard of it (Johnsen 2005: 35).

Laila Spik confirmed that the term was persistently used in her childhood by her originally Lule-Sámi father and (in other words) by her Northern -Sámi mother. She translated it as "one with nature." It meant a type of pleasant feeling or an awareness that one was acting in harmony with the spirits of the surrounding area, such as animal and plant spirits. To ask for permission ritually was a way of achieving *oktavuohta luondui* – cooperation to the mutual benefit of all beings. She also knew the other meaning of the word as a basic trait or characteristic of an individual, but confirmed that the other use, as general non-human surroundings, was also a way of using the term.

The *oktavuohta luondui* was a type of inner guidance that resulted from contact on the level of thought with a personified nature of non-human persons who in turn guided humans' behavior towardthem. The aim was to have a respectful mutual relationship and an ecologically sustainable use of resources. To live on the basis of the principle of *oktavuohta luondui* was incompatible with the "new life," meaning the life in modernized Sámi society, according to Laila Spik (May 2013).

I conclude that according to my limited research the term *luondu* was in some areas traditionally used for designating ecosystems but might have been used in different places by different families in different ways. The sources that confirmed a usage of the natural environment as expressed in the word *luondu* as an overarching concept also closely linked it to a type of permission-ritual that was taught them in their pre-1970s childhood and which still serves as a guiding principle for concrete behavior.

The way Tore Bongo and the young woman I heard talking about it use the feeling of *oktavuohta luondui* are the only examples of a traditional ritual that integrates the question linked to the use of modern technology. It might

---

119 "Luonddujiena guldalit."

lead people to oppose new mining sites and for instance brought Tore Bongo to reduce his use of motorized vehicles while also growing to dislike airtravel.

This non-human personhood attributed to "nature" leads to identification, empathy, commitment and well-being and significantly helps to induce respect for the restraint and strict behavioral rules that ecologically respectful behaviour might sometimes require.

7.2 Mother Earth

One of the Northern Sámi terms for land or landscape is *eatnan*, which is etymologically closely related to *eatni* meaning "mother." In ancient Sámi religion there is no information of any kind about Mother Earth as a subject with superhuman agency. Kerstin Eidlitz Kuoljok (1999) has written about the absence of a generalized Mother Earth cult in Sámi religions. She discusses the concept of Mother Earth in various Siberian traditions and found many goddesses called "mothers" in various religious traditions. However, in all the cultures she researched there is no overarching concept for a cultish divinity like Mother Earth. She agrees with the Swedish scholar of religious studies O. Pettersson (1967) who concluded that a worship of a Mother Earth as a separate goddess has never existed, but that it was and is in use as a metaphorical image. The idea of a Mother Earth cult was created by scholars in the mid-twentieth century by building upon badly conceived theories of Taylor, according to the American researcher Gill in 1987 (Eidlitz Kuoljok 1999: 194).

The discussion does not end here, as there is more to say about mothers and the beliefs attached to them. In ancient Sámi religion the place where the goddesses who carry the names of *akka* or *áhkku* (woman or grandmother) is the air. *Maddar-akka* is a personification of the middle level of air or she is told to live there; her three daughters *Sarakka*, *Ugsakka* and *Juksakka* live in the lowest levels of air just above the earth. *Sarakka* lived next to the fireplace and *Uksahka* and *Juksakka* next to the entrance of a dwelling (Skanke quoted in Rydving 1995: 123, 135). They were responsible for the formation of human and animal bodies and their health and physical well-being. *Sarakka* is the central female goddess to whom all Sámi addressed themselves regarding their daily problems and for whom they made daily offerings to the fireplace (Anonymous in Leem and Skanke quoted in Rydving 1995: 98, 129, 130).

For Louise Bäckman (1984) and Myrhaug (1997: 89) *Maddar-akka* is a variant of a universally worshipped "Great Mother." This is an analysis that is not supported by Kuoljok Eidlitz, as mentioned earlier. There are also celestial female deities like *Rana nieda* who was held responsible for the production of matter, like the growing of grass.

Metaphorical references to land and nature as a mother are frequent. Turi says in one text that the earth and the water are our mother and that God is our father (1920: 117). As to Sámi literature, Nils-Aslak Valkeapää's (1943–2001) last poetry book from 2001 has the title *Eanni, eannázan* (*Earth, My Mother*).

On 22 February 1998 in Karasjok/Finnmark a global proclamation entitled "The Karasjok Declaration" was formulated by indigenous representatives from twenty countries and five continents who were members of Lutheran churches united by the World Council of Churches. The declaration has as its main theme the importance of the participants' relationship to Mother Earth and their sacred land and territories, this in turn seen as being directly linked to their cultural survival. Mother Earth becomes an overarching term for concern regarding the ecological threat.

> We are deeply conscious of our relationship with our Mother, the Earth, and the sacredness of our land and territories. We reaffirmed that our identity, cultures, languages, philosophy of life, and our spirituality are linked to the balanced relationship with all of creation. This relationship has ensured our continued existence in spite of oppression, exploitation and attempted assimilation by dominant socioeconomic-politico-cultural and religious entities. (...) Our faith is that we are upheld by the Spirit of God and that all things are in the hands of our Creator. This vision gives us strength and direction in our struggle for the survival of the earth, our Mother (The Karasjok Declaration 1998).

What is interesting about this declaration is that lands and territories are called sacred but not Mother Earth. The balance and the survival of the indigenous peoples is seen as threatened by a number of ecological problems like "mining, wildlife conservation, logging, hydro-electric dams, militarization, eco-tourism and other projects." As to the demands, they mainly concern the protection of indigenous people's overall rights and that they be listened to, respected and supported in all aspects of church life. There is no mention of any demand for the integration of belief concepts or change or symbolism and liturgies or separate indigenous bodies or even indigenous congregations inside churches.

To conclude, the concept of Mother Earth is an ancient and traditional Sámi concept but one that is neither sacralized by Sámi tradition nor does it have a clearly defined supernatural personhood with rituals attached to it. The word "sacred" in connection with *Mother Earth* is avoided, as also in the newly adopted United Nation resolution on' Mother Earth Day.[120] Still, the concept is to a high degree used as a key metaphor for calling on more action to achieve ecological sustainability linked to the modern challenges of modern technology and globalization.

7.3 Ancient Pantheon[121]

The gods and goddesses of the ancient Sámi pantheon(s) were distributed over various levels of existence, which described their physical emplacement in the universe. The belief system in most areas might have had five levels, others three. For some areas, the levels are reflected in the regionally determined horizontal-level patterns of the drawings on the drums.[122] For others like the southern Sámi drums, that have the symbol of the sun the middle and no horizontal levels, it is not. Despite the absence of the levels on these drum paintings, the ancient missionaries recorded that the southern Sámi also had gods and goddesses at various cosmic locations: from the underground to the ether and in the "over-heavens," a far-away place in the cosmos.[123] In the appendix to this chapter, I have undertaken an overview of the main gods and goddesses, the places where they are located and their functions.

The gods and goddesses had the explicit power to protect and strengthen the functioning of the cosmos, the ecosystems and all living beings on earth. At the same time the humans had a responsibility in worshipping the main

---

120 The day is on 22 April. The United Nations' Resolution adopted by the General Assembly on 22 April 2009 on International Mother Earth Day: "Recognizing that Mother Earth is a common expression for the planet earth in a number of countries and regions, which reflects the interdependence that exists among human beings, other living species and the planet we all inhabit."

121 See apppendix for a schematic overview of the pantheon.

122 To study the various regionial types of the about ancient 70 drums that were confiscated in the time of forced christianization see Christoffersson (2010), Manker (1938).

123 See Rydving (2010: 69) for areas that the missionaries described, also Skanke; and Rydving (1995: 123) for the division of divinities into five levels.

god to keep the cosmos intact as well as the other deities in order to ensure their favorable actions.

A pantheon of gods and goddesses at five levels has been mostly described by Danish/Norwegian missionary writings from the early eighteenth century. It is not always clear what area they cover, as the missionaries did not distinguish between the various Sámi cultural areas. They often traveled long distances to convert Sámi and/or held office at various stages in their lives. Some of the best-known authors copied almost literally large parts of each other's writings (Rydving 1995). Missionary Isaac Olsen – who worked at the same time and in the same area as the *noaide* Anders Poulsen with his well-known five-level drum – did not mention these five levels in his important record of Sámi religion.

According to a selection of significant fragments which Rydving (1995) has compared in a synopsis, Sámi distinguish the following five levels: those highest up in the starry heavens, heavenly gods in the sky, in the lower skies just above the earth, underground gods that live a bit below the earth, and those living deep down inside earth (Mebius 2007: 63, Rydving 1995: 76). There are variations in the way their special placement is described.

The gods and goddesses could be of two different natures. They were either literal personifications of natural phenomena like the sun and the moon, the different layers of sky and air and lightning, or they were principles or "forces" that ruled in nature like the "lord of the animals," the god responsible for the creation of souls, the principle of conception or the creation of animal and human bodies. They could also be both. The sun (Mebius 2007 quotes A. Westman 1997: 77) could be at the same time an astral body with a non-human personhood and in that capacity the ancestor of the Sámi and the principle of life-giving warmth. Most gods and goddesses have some task that isrelated to the functioning of ecosystems: they dwell in parts of it, they can be identical with certain parts of the cosmos or the earthly ecosystems, or they have a decisive power over it by ruling and balancing the cosmos and the earthly ecosystems.

As to the sources for the ancient pantheon, they are mainly accounts from priests and missionaries from the sixteenth to the nineteenth centuries along with fragments of information about gods and goddesses recorded up until the early twentieth century, for instance by Itkonen. Only very sporadic contemporary living traditions have been recorded.

132

Living Traditions of Gods and Goddesses Today

In my interviews and visits, I have encountered two living traditions related to ancient gods. The god *Rota* was mentioned in the Lule Sámi area, according to Marit Myrvoll. Families used to put a bowl with water in the house on Christmas night to make sure that *Rota* would not harm anyone in the house (MM Nov. 2012). As to *Sarakka*. some traditional Lule and southern Sámi are still every day pouring drops of drink into the fire or onto the soil, thanking her for providing food and safety (Jernsletten 2004, LS Aug. 2012). Laila Spik also grew up with references to *Rota* as a deity to which one should be attentive (Bornstein 2002: 108).

Ecological Aspects of *Radien* and the Antler-God

The ruler *Radien*[124] lives in the highest starry heavens and is not only the overall creator, holding the cosmos in place and creating human souls, but also the main god responsible for the growth and protection of reindeer. Some missionaries wrote about an under-god or equivalent to *Radien*, the Horngod *Tjåervienraedie*, who had the largest influence on the reindeer herds (Leem quoted in Mebius 2007: 64, Holmberg 1915/1987: 51) and who also made everything grow (J. Kildal quoted in Mebius 2007: 65). For Randulf he is responsible for good fishing results and the reproduction of reindeer (Randulf quoted by Mebius 2007: 65). He is sometimes the equivalent of the divinity *Veralden olmai* or *Storjunckeren*.

Just like the pointing world pillars, the horns and the pillar symbolize male fertility. Horns and male reindeer genitals are sacrificed to him (Mebius 2007: 64) (Holmberg 1915/1987: 51–54).

J. Kildal describes his cosmic role as the god who supports the "world pillar" that links the earth to the cosmos (Mebius 2007: 147). His sacred symbol and offering site was often a reversed dead tree: a tree stump placed with the roots up in the air (Mebius 2007: 64). The pillar is supposed to uphold the skies, and its weakening can cause the heavens descend. Humans must sacrifice actively in order to make sure that the cosmic order is maintained, otherwise the skies could collapse on them.

---

124 For an overview of references to *Radien* in key missionary writings, see Rydving (1995: 67–68); for a summary, see Mebius (2007: 64–69).

Ecological Aspects of *Ruona-nieda or Rana-nieda*

The green maiden, spring maiden or reindeer-calf woman,[125] *Ruona nieida*, was also part of the upper echelon of cosmic gods. For Von Westen, *Rana nieida* was the most important of all goddesses (Mebius 2007: 124). Her responsibility was to make all trees and herbs grow green in springtime in order to provide food for reindeer and other animals. Sacrifices are made to make sure the reindeer obtain grass and reach the mountains in good time during the spring (Holmberg 1915/1987: 49, Kulonen 2005: 281). For Skanke, she is called either "Rana nieida," "Radiennieda" or "Blenen." "Blenen" is also a name for the aromatic plant Angelica Archangelica, which was an important herb for healing and a food for both reindeer and humans (Skanke quoted in Rydving 1995: 170) (Mebius 2007: 125). For Skanke, *Horagallis* and *Rana-nieida* take care of reindeer. She is described as corresponding to the "spirit/mother of plants/verdure/grass" in Ter and Kildin in the (Eastern) Sámi tradition (Holmberg 1915/1987: 50, Kulonen 2005: 281).

Leibolmai

Leibolmai is designated as "God of grasslands" (Anonymous in Leem, quoted in Rydving 1995: 92) and provides good luck in hunting (Leem, Sidenius, Forbes, S. Kildal) especially in catching bears;[126] Skanke calls *Leibolmai* "skov-guder," which is forest gods in plural (Skanke quoted in Rydving 1995: 172, Mebius 2007: 94–96), as opposed to the water-gods, "Sjatze-olmai." For some he is the "bear-man" or "alder tree-man" who protects wild animals and especially bears but who can also make humans catch them (Randulf quoted in Holmberg 1915/1987: 74).

For some the name *Leibolmai* is related to *laibi* (bread); S. Kildal, quoted by Rydving, calls him "Brödmanden" or Bread Man (1995: 92); for others he is related to the 'lieibi', the alder tree bark that is used, for instance, to

---

125 For an overview of references to *Rana nieida* in key missionary writings, see Rydving 1995: 70, 71; for a summary, see Mebius 2007: 124–127; also see Holmberg 1915/1987: 49–50).

126 For an overview of references to *Leibolmai* in key missionary writings, see Rydving (1995: 69); for a summary, see Mebius (2007: 94–96).

produce red coloring for leather skins. The alder tree was considered sacred (Bäckman 1991: 19 quoting Paproth).

According to an anonymous party at Leem this was the deity that Sámi pray to most. I suppose that he meant the Sámi male, as hunting and rituals to achieve hunting luck were normally their domain. They prayed and praised him with songs at morning and evening (quoted in Rydving 1995: 92). As to underscore *Leibolmai*'s importance, the missionaries compare him and *Sarahkka* in a way to Jesus, saying that Sámi drink the blood and eat the body of *Sarahkka*, and some the body of *Leibolmai* (Anonymous at Leem, Sidenius, Forbus, S. Kildal quoted by Rydving 1995: 96).[127]

Other Gods Relevant to Ecology

Another god of importance is *Beive* the sun god. *Beive* provides the warmth necessary to make grass grow and reindeer calves live and is denoted as the mother of all animals. The symbol that was used at many sun sacrifices was a ring of twigs or a brass metal ring (Rheen quoted in Mebius 2007: 75–79 quoting Rheen, Lundius, S. Kildal, Lundius and others, Holmberg 1915/1987: 54–56). The sun was also seen as an ancestor of the Sámi, they calling themselves "descendents of the sons of the sun" in an ancient epic song recorded by a priest, Anders Fjellner in the Northern Sámi area in Sweden in the mid-nineteenth century (Kulonen 2005: 32). Gods can also have destructive powers, like *Horagallis* when he produces thunder that uproots trees or disperses reindeer, and *Bieggolmai* who is the god of wind and the waters. There is a "climate" god, *Gisen* or *Gissen-olmai/Jisjienålmaj*: "Gissen olmai is also a god for wind and weather, snow and ice. The Lapps have given him offerings so that snow and ice will end and not damage them."[128] (Anonymous at Leem, Sidenius, Forbus quoted in Rydving 1995: 85, 87 119,

---

127 "Andre have ædt Veraldne Rads Legem og drukket Sar Achas blod, efterdi disse to skabe et fuldkomment Menneske, den ene Legemet, den andre Sjælen." ["Others have eaten the body of Veralde and drunk Sárákká's blood because these two shape a complete human, the one the body, the other the soul."] (S. Kildal quoted in Rydving 1995: 96–7).

128 "Gissen olmai er og en gud för vind og väder, snö og ijs, Lapperna har givet honom offer at sno og is skulle uphöra og icke wara dem til skadas (Anonymous at Leem, Sidenius, Forbus quoted in Rydving 1995: 85, 87 119, Holmberg 1915/1987: 65–66).

Holmberg 1915/1987: 65–66). The Sámi must also sacrifice to him in order to make sure that weather conditions, like the freezing of snow to ice, do not damage reindeer and that the cold season ceases in good time.

Ecological Sustainability and the Ancient Pantheon

The entire universe including the earth was personified and composed and inhabited by non-human persons who possessed their own personalities and agency. They created life, made the vegetation grow, regulated the climate and weather and had many other concrete tasks. The divinities were guardians of respect for the traditional nature-related value system. This view leads to an identification with the cosmos and the earth. Humans are becoming a part of a dynamic cosmic network of mutual relationships.

Both the sun and the moon are said to have children who intermarry with Sámi. Sámi therefore have a mythic cosmic origin. The sun is also seen as the mother to all animals. Herein lies a confusion of identities between humans and the cosmos, and there is also the idea of having a common origin with animals.

The god of the wild animals, *Leibolmai*, is not too surprisingly designated as the central and most worshipped god. He had to provide safe daily food supplies. The focus of gods and goddesses often lies in the animal and vegetable resources used for nourishment and survival. In the text that I studied there was little mention of any concern for the general well-being of creatures that do not have any utilitarian value other than to keep the heavens in the skies and the entire world safe by virtue of that ritual.

Worshipping deities was considered necessary to regulating the relationship between humans and the natural environment so as to guarantee stable natural conditions. Humans had a responsibility to maintain the order of the world. They had to behave well by respecting the rules of behavior and thereby please the gods so as to make sure that the grass kept growing, that the weather was not damaging life, that the wild animals and reindeer could reproduce, and so forth. Worship and sacrifice in collective rituals expressed the collective commitment of many different Sámi communities and larger cultural groups. This can be seen as the ideal of maintaining ecological sustainability, since humans had an important responsibility in keeping the ecosystems functioning well.

Chapter 8 – Conclusions

From this study it has become clear that there were indeed a series of powerful mechanisms that worked toward ecological sustainability in the traditional Sámi religious culture, even if Sámi today do not live more ecologically sustainable lives than the average citizen in the states where they reside. I will summarize the type of mechanisms that I researched, categorized according to the type of belief, ritual or narrative they represent, before relating them to general aspects of religion in order to convey a better understanding of their role in the cultural system. Finally, I will make some concluding remarks and suggest what the traditional Sámi belief system can tell us with regard to today's ecological crisis.

Religious Mechanisms for Ecological Sustainability

The first religious mechanism is the interchangeability of identity between humans and non-humans. A human can become an animal or can marry one and beget children. The physical form is very relative and fluid, for instance by shape-shifting (ch. 4.1), animal ancestry (ch. 5.1) and marriage with underground spirits (ch. 6.1) and even divinities like the sun had the status of an ancestor (ch. 7.3). We find this concept of interchangeable identity also in the way that some Sámi understand the role of the traditional chant, the Yoik, in which the singer can become a landscape[129] or create a landscape by singing about it. This mechanism has not only a historical and mythological dimension, as in ancient stories about women marrying bears or reindeer, but according to my two informants, animal ancestry is a living concept to this very day, both of them having mentioned the hare as a (potential) ancestor.

---

129 "A yoik is not merely a description; it attempts to capture its subject in its entirety: it's like a holographic, multi-dimensional living image, a replica, not just a flat photograph or simple visual memory. It is not about something, it is that something. It does not begin and it does not end. A yoik does not need to have words – its narrative is in its power, it can tell a life story in song." Ursula Länsman: "Sami Culture and the Yoik," FolkWorld, no. 9, May 1999. For Harald Gaski on the change of perspective in the yoik text, see "The Secretive Text: Yoik Lyrics as Literature and Tradition," *Nordlit*, no. 5, Nov. 2000.

With reference to its effects on ecological sustainability, the interchange-ability of identity leads to a set of attitudes and emotions that are favorable for envisioning sustainable behavior: first of all interest, observation, sympathy, empathy, identification, a feeling of friendship; these attitudes can stimulate the will to take responsibility in caring for non-humans and become integrated into a person's identity. They can result in a willingness to protect the habitat and make sure that its creatures thrive. According to my ecological interpretation of the underground spirits, this interchangeability breaks down the boundary between human and the "other," in this case animals or the personification of the soil. The ecosystem is not "alien" or "other." Contact with animals that also could be you or your relative becomes a positive factor in a person's identity.

The mechanism of attributing non-human personhood is a principle applied on every level: individual animals, species up to entire local ecosystems like a lake or a hunting ground, landscape, and in the end the whole of "nature" is filled with non-human persons. The non-human person becomes a superhuman agent and the communion with him is a ritualized activity playing an invaluable role in the maintenance of ecological sustainability (ch. 4.2).

The concept of non-human personhood on the level of entire animal species is particularly effective in enhancing ecological sustainability. This shows that there is an awareness of the biological needs of species and a well-developed sense of the functioning of ecosystems in which various species, each needing their niche, try to survive as well as they can.

Attributing non-human personhood is a way to conceptualize one's relationship with the outside world, which implies similar effects on emotional-behavioral attitudes, as mentioned under the previous points. The human universe becomes an entirely different place, reminiscent of a fairy tale come true; there are no mechanical objects, no coincidences, everything is subjective and every event has an intention. The universe is entirely alive.

Probably the most powerful ritual instruments for ecological sustainability encountered in this research are the permission- rituals. They can be performed with any non-human, such as trees (ch. 4.2), bears (ch. 5.1), underground spirits (ch. 6.1) or even vis-à-vis "nature" as a whole (ch. 7.1). There are different forms of ritualistic communication, and in the case that the answer is "no," the human will abstain from the planned action. This ritual imposes clear limitations on the use of natural resources.

Sacrifices to *sieidi* or gods seem to be constructed in ways that interact with what one might term the ecosystem in the pre-Christian religious context. Such rituals are no longer frequently performed today but they remain an underlying presence beneath other forms, like paying respect to or greeting a holy mountain or a *sieidi*; or at least not disturbing it. The *sieidis* are supposed to watch over the sustainable management of a location with a specific resource, like a fishing lake, to make sure the resources do not become depleted or disturbed (ch. 6.2). The required sacrifice for the extraction of resources can be seen as a form of contractual engagement with superhuman agency ensuring that both sides will respect the traditional set of rules which impose ecologically suitable behavior and reciprocity.

The authority of the various superhuman agents is based on their power to impose sanctions. The sanction mostly takes the form of symbolic consequences that erroneous behavior would have induced in the long term if the sanction had not put an immediate stop to the behavior. In traditional society the survival of a community depended on the good condition of its local resources. The health of people and in particular of children depended on good drinking water. By preserving the frogs, which are supposed to keep the well clean, one keeps the children healthy. Teasing frogs can make children sick (ch. 5.2). A Christianized version of sanctions is expressed by such phrases as "the animals and trees will witness those who abuse them on Judgment Day" (ch. 4.2).

The informants did not consider traditional beliefs to be scary or frightening; on the contrary, these beliefs gave them a sensation of predictability and safety. They had a strong nostalgia for them and remembered times when they felt safe and happy, which they call "the round life." The provision of safety through the religious mechanisms was obviously much stronger than the fear of any possible sanctions.

The nature of the relationship with non-human persons is not exclusively friendly and polite, with the occasional friendly trickster causing short-term minor problems; that is obviously the ideal situation. In real life there can be killing and abuse, fighting, or neglect (ch. 4.2). The presence of mythological narratives allows for the conclusion of mutual agreements with clear commitments.

Superhuman agents like the *sieidi* or *háldi* but also mythological narratives have become mediators for a set of rules which ensure the sustainable use of natural resources for an entire community and entire families from an intergenerational perspective.

Relation to the Overall Theoretical Concepts of Religion

Emplacement is a central factor in understanding Sámi religious beliefs. Fundamental in every ritual is delimitation of the spatial dimension while linked to a concept of rights of exclusive use. Fishing is done in a specific place, permission is asked from a specific tree. The dependency on the ecosystem here is immediate, extremely concrete and clearly observable.

As to embodiment, the human body is a key factor in the religious practices. The religion regulates access to places and food provision, and these actions often concern the body in terms of hunger, sickness or imposed death. The body also becomes an instrument in rituals, like in the ritual where a person "feels" with his body whether the answer is yes or no. The aim of life is to maintain it, the *birgejupmi*. The living body is at the center of attention.

The separation between the visible and the invisible is clearly related to the Sámi traditional worldview. It corresponds to the criticism of Talal Asad and others of the European way in which "religion" has been redefined. The informants showed a clear awareness of the functionality of their beliefs and of their own construction of at least a part of them. The *sieidi* is chosen and consecrated by humans and, if it does not work, they also can destroy it and choose a new one (ch. 6.2). Even if the people I interviewed might doubt the physical existence of a *máddo* or an underground spirit that they clearly considered a creation of the human imagination, the communications with non-humans was not questioned in the same way.

For Sámi the world consists of a web of relationships between non-humans and humans, and it does not make much sense to single out something like "nature" as a focal point. In this way the mysticism of "nature," as in European Romanticism, is alien to them. Nature has its own value, just like anything else, but it is not idealized. What probably surprises is that nature is taken fully into the web of equal relations and becomes the object of empathic relations. This is an element, which still is alien to the dominant contemporary society, and it might provoke strong reactions.

The concept of fluid identities questions the one-person/one-soul concept. I was reluctant to use the concept of animism in describing these religious traditions. In my opinion there are still unanswered theoretical questions in the nature of the fluid identity and in what this means for the concept of the soul and various forms of superhuman powers.

Religious expression via the actions of the superhuman agents becomes a culturally determined system of representation that adresses the collective needs of an ecologically sustainable management of the ecosystem.

Ongoing adaptation of Sámi traditional culture in modern globalized society is an interesting process to observe. Only a few ancient rituals were shown to include modern technology and wider areas. The system was based on a small-scale economy where each community took its own full share of responsibility for its monument over an extended period of time. They expected the others to do the same. To put it simply, every local community minded his own business. One does not know how the ancient pantheon functioned and whether it included the creation of larger solidarities, like seasonal feasts, which implied gatherings on larger regional levels.

Unsurprisingly the principles of sustainability were only in very few cases applied to the national or global economy. From the start they seem to have been limited to self-governed areas in a cultural space in which groups of people, called 'siidda' were living in self-sufficiency. Traditional Sámi are bound to their area through many different types of local superhuman agents. Even the dead live either under the ground or in the local sacred mountains. What modern ecological moral can be learned from the traditional Sámi about how to achieve an ecologically sustainable management of natural resources? In the traditional Sámi society, dependency on ecosystems was local, existential and based on extensive knowledge of all aspects of it. Can human ethics handle the transition from the local to the global level?

In general the boundaries between religion, values and ideals are very attenuated in post-secular European society. Religions have a stable place in the global culture because new religious expressions are arising in many places, many of them outside of institutionalized churches. Religion is at the same time the expression of a cultural system; it contributes to the continuous reconstruction of it. Religion is not expected to disappear, as was thought and hoped for by segments of European society ever since the Enlightenment. But opinions diverge with respect to the role of religion in ecological sustainability. Religious organizations and their ideas do not have unanimous support in European society. They are not always seen as having a positive or a relevant role. The policymaking is based on non-religious strategies to manage resources in an ecologically sustainable manner. A better integration of traditional ecological knowledge, that might include spiritual aspects, in the decisionmaking processes will hopefully lead to more effective management of biodiversity. Desirable would be better legal protection of landscape sites that are considered sacred by Sámi and a better integration of respect for religious traditions in measures for the protection of nature.

Second, it is necessary to have a more concrete awareness of our factual dependency on ecosystems and thus develop our knowledge with regard to keeping them intact and productive. User groups should be clearly delimited so that that extraction can be directly related to consumption. The system must be strictly maintained and transgressions have to be directly sanctioned.

And third, there is the factor of motivation, which makes respect for the rules of ecological sustainability and management a special experiences that gives meaning to life. Identification with and engagement in empathic communication with personified ecosystems – or even the total blurring of one's identity with them – might have very positive motivational effects leading to mutually beneficial relationships and a sustainable future for coming generations.

Summary in Norwegian

Kartlegging av økologisk bærekraftighet i samiske tradisjonelle trosfore-stillinger og ritualer.

Denne studien har som målsetting å lage en oversiktsanalyse av samiske religiøse trosforestillinger ritualer og fortellinger som kan settes i sammenheng med en økologisk bærekraftig forvalting av økosystemer i det tradisjonelle samiske samfunnet. Arealet omfatter det hele samiske området med vekt på det nord-samiske. Samer i dag lever like økologisk bærekraftig som den gjennomsnittlige befolkningen. Nesten ingen av de gamle ritualer, ble knyttet til bruk av moderne teknologi. I det moderne samfunnet har religion en annen rolle enn i det tradisjonelle samiske. Studien er ikke sammenlignende, og mange av de beskrevne religiøse uttrykk kan beskrives også i nabokulturene. Mitt ønske er å bidra til en mer informert og nyansert debatt om samisk identitet og økologisk bærekraftighet. Som kilder bruker jeg historisk sekundærlitteratur og primærkilder som intervjuer. Trosforestillinger som er undersøkt er inndelt i fire romslige nivåer: fra det individuelle, til artsnivået, til det lokale og til slutt det globale.

Religiøse uttrykk som jeg har beskrevet og analysert inkluderer kommunikasjon blant annet i form av tillatelse-ritualer med ikke-menneskelige personer, respekt og offer til hellige sted, religiøse sanksjoner, mytiske avtaler mellom mennesker, dyr og økosystemer hvor gjensidige forholdsregler blir videreført, og en sakralisering av naturen og identifisering med dyr og en generalisert intersubjektivitet hvor identitet mellom mennesker og omgivelsen smelter sammen.

De tradisjonelle trosforestillingene hadde som mål å opprettholde de naturlige balanse lokalsamfunnene var avhengige av, men de var bunnet til eksklusive bruksrettigheter og en økonomi basert på selvberging av små lokale samfunn med de lokale økosystemene som eneste ressursgrunnlag. Når samfunnet forandret seg, forsvant også den største delen av religiøsiteten som var direkte knyttet til konkrete handlingene.

References

Aas, Ø., Øian, H., Waaler, R. & Skår, M, 2010. **Allmennhetens bruk av utmarka i Finnmark** NINA Rapport 642: 94, Norsk institutt for naturforskning (NINA), Lillehammer.

Andersen, Oddmund. 2005. **Fiskemáddo-fiskenes stammor, I** Bårjås, Árran., Tysfjord, Norway, p. 71–75.

Appfel-Marglin, Frederique, 2011. **Subversive Spiritualities: How Rituals Enact the World,** Oxford University Press.

Asad, Talal 2003. **Formations of the Secular: Christianity, Islam, Modernity.** Stanford: Stanford University Press.

Bäckman, L., 1984. **The Akkas. A study of four goddesses in the religion of the Saamis.** I: W. i: Tyloch (red.): **Current Progress in the Methodology of the Science of Religions.** Warsaw. p. 31–39.

Bäckman, Louise, 1975. **Sávja: Föreställingar om hjälp-og skyddsväsen i heliga fjäll bland samerna,** Acta Universitatis Stockholmiensis, Almquist & Wiksell Stockholm.

Bäckman, Louise, 1991. The Master of the Animal, on Hunting Rites Among the Saami, in: **Hunting Rituals of the Northern Peoples: 5**[th] **International Abashiri Symposium,** Feb. 20–22, 1991 in Japan, p. 17–24.

Bell, Catherine, 1992. **Ritual Theory, Ritual Practice,** Oxford University Press.

Bell, Catherine, 1997. **Ritual Perspectives and Dimensions,** Oxford University Press.

Bergstrøm, Grete Gunn, 2001. **Tradisjonell kunnskap og sámisk modernitet, en studie av vilkår for tilegnelse av tradisjonell kunnskap i en moderne sámisk samfunnskontekst,** hovedoppgave Institutt for pedagogikk UIT.

Bientie, Bierna 2003. **Det er landet som eier folket.** Part of Svenska kyrkan 2003. Samisk kyrka nu är rätt tid för praktisk solidaritet med samerna p. 22–30.

Bird Rose, Deborah, 2002. **Sacred site, ancestral clearing, and environmental ethics,** in Harvey Graham (ed.), 2002. Readings in Indigenous Religions, Continuum New York, p. 319.

Bornstein, Anna, med Laila Spik, 2002. **Den samiske vandringsrösten, -Jag är kunskapen,** Svenska forlaget.

Brightman, Marc, Grotti, Vanessa Elisa, Ulturgasheva, Olga, 2012. Animism in Rainforest and Tundra, Personhood, Animals, Plants and Things in Contemporary Amazonia and Siberia, Berghahn books New York, Oxford.

Christensen, Cato, 2010. Religion i Veiviseren: En analyse av samisk religiøs revitalisering, DIN: Religionsvitenskapelig tidsskrift 2010 (1–2), p. 6–33.

Christoffersson, Rolf, 2010. Med tre röster og tusende bilder, Om den sámiske trumman, Uppsala universitetet.

Fangen, Katrine 2004. Deltagende observasjon, Fagbokforlaget Bergen, Norway.

Fellman, Jacob 1844/1906. Anteckninger under min vistelse i Lappmarken 1–4 Helsingfors, Finska Litteratursällskapets tryckeri.

Fikret Berkes, 1999/2012. Sacred Ecology, Routledge.

Fjellström, Pehr, comment by Louise Bäckman, 1981. Facsimile 1755: Kort Berättelse om Lapparnas Björna-Fänge, Samt Deras der Wid Brukade Widskeppelser, Norrländska skrifter nr 5, Två Bokforläggare Bokforlag, Umeå.

Fonneland, Trude A. 2010: Samisk nysjamanisme: urfolksspiritualitet mellom lokale og globale straumar. Tidsskrift for kulturforskning 2010; Volum 9 (3) s. 5–18, UiB.

Geertz, Armin, 2004. Can We Move Beyond Primitivism? On Recovering the Indigenes of Indigenous Religion in The Academic Study of Religion. In Olupona Jacob K, Beyond Primitivism, Indigenous religious traditions and modernity, ed. p. 37–70.

Geertz, Clifford, 1966. Religion as a Cultural System. In: Michael Banton (ed.), Anthropological Approaches to the Study of Religion, London: Tavistock. ASA Monographs 3, p. 1–46.

Gilhus, Anne Ingvild S; Mikaelsson, Lisbeth. 2007. Verdens levende religioner, Pax Forlag Oslo.

Grim and Tucker, 2002. Intellectual and Organizational Foundations of Religion and Ecology, in in: Bauman, Whitney A. Bohannon II Richard R., O'Brien Kevin, 2011, Grounding Religion, A Field Guide to the Study of Religions and Ecology, Routledge London, p. 81–95.

Guttorm, Gunvor, 2011. Árbediehtu (Sami traditional knowledge) – as a concept and in practice.

Hallowell A. Irving, 2002/1960. Ojibwa Ontology, Behavior and World-View in Harvey, Graham (ed.) **Readings in Indigenous Religions,** Continuum London, p. 17–49.

Hansen Lars- Ivar, Olsen Bjørnar, 2004. **Samenes historie fram til 1750.** Cappelen Damm, Oslo.

Harvey, Graham, 2006. **Animism, Respecting the Living World,** London, UK, Hurst.

Helander – Renvall Elina, 1999. **Sami Subsistence Activities—Spatial Aspects and Structuration,** Acta Borealia: A Nordic Journal of Circumpolar Societies, 16:2, p. 7–25.

Helander Elina, 2001. Samiska rättsuppfattninger i Tana, i: **Samiska sedvaner og rättsoppfattningar** in: Norges offentlige utredninger, NOU 2001: 34. Kapittel 6.1.

Helander, Elina (ed.), 1996. **Awakened Voice, The Return of Sami knowledge,** Dieđut 1996: 4, Nordic Sami institute.

Henriksen, John B. 2011. Working with Traditional Knowledge: Communities, Institutions, Information Systems, Law and Ethics. In: **Writings from the Árbediehtu Pilot Project on Documentation and Protection of Sami Traditional Knowledge. Dieđut 1/2011.** Sámi allaskuvla / Sámi University College. p. 77–97.

Holmberg-Harva, Uno; Boreman, Per, Wiklund, Karl Bernhard; 1915/1987. **Lapparnas religion.** I Uppsala multiethnic papers, 10, Uppsala universitet.

Hughes, Aaron W., 2012. Boundary Maintainance: Religions as organic-cultural flows: on Thomas Tweed, Crossings and Dwellings. in. Stausberg M. (ed)., **Contemporary Theories of Religion A Critical Compagnion,** Routledge.

Hultkrantz, Åge, 1966. **In memory of Ivar Paulson,** in Temenos vol. 2, 1966, p. 183–187.

Hultkrantz, Åge, 1994. Religion and Environment among the Saami: An Ecological study. in: Irimoto Takashi and Yamada Takao 1994, **Circumpolar Religion and Ecology, An Antropology of the North,** University of Tokyo press p. 347–374.

Hultkrantz, Åge, 2000. Fifty Years of Research on Sámi Folklore and Mythology, in: Pentikäinen Juha, 2000, **Sámi Folkloristics,** NNF publications 6, Åbo University p. 75–102.

Itkonen, T.I., 1946. **Heidnische Religion und späterer Aberglaube bei den finnischen Lappen,** Mémoires de la société finno-ungroise, Helsinki.

Jenkins, Wills, 2011. Sustainability, in: Bauman, Whitney A. Bohannon II Richard R.

Jernsletten, Jorunn, 2002. **Landskap of religiøsitet i et sørsamisk perspektiv slektsbånd og offerskikker, fra Samisk forhistorie: rapport fra konferanse Lakselv 5–6 september 2002,** p. 113–122.

Jernsletten, Jorunn 2004. **Landskap som tekst og handelende** subject Lars Magne Andreassen (red). i: Dieđut 2004–5, Samiske landskapsstudier, rapport fra et arbeidsseminar.

Johnsen, Tore, 2005. **Sámi luondduteologiija, Samisk naturteologi – på grunnlag av nålevende tradisjonsstoff og nedtegnede myter,** Institutt for religionsvitenskap Universitetet i Tromsø.

Johnsen, Tore, 2007. **Jordens barn, solens barn, vindens barn : kristen tro i et samisk landskap,** Verbum.

Juergensmeyer, Mark, Wade Clark Roof, 2012. **Encyclopedia of Global Religion,** ed. Sage.

Kalstad, Johan Albert, 1997. **Slutten på trommetiden.** I: Ottar nr 217, 1997–4, Noaidier og trommer, -Samiske religiøse tradisjoner fra vår nære fortid. Tromsø Museum, p. 16–27.

Kraft, Siv Ellen, 2004. **Et Hellig fjell blir til- Om samer, OL og arktisk magi,** i Nytt Norsk Tidsskrift 2004 (Årg. 21, nr 3/4), Universitetsforlaget, p. 238–249.

Kraft, Siv Ellen, 2007. **Natur, Spiritualitet og Tradisjon, om akademisk romantisering og feilslåtte primitivisme oppgjør,** i DIN Religionsvitenskapelig tidsskrift 2007 (1), Tromsø, p. 53–62.

Kraft, Siv Ellen, 2009. **Sami Indigenous Spirituality: Religion and Nation-building in Norwegian Sapmi.** Temenos 2009; Volum 45 (2). p. 179–206.

Krech III Shepard, 2000. **The Ecological Indian: Myth and History,** W.W. Norton and comp. New York.

Krupnik, Igor, 1993. **Arctic Adaptations. Native Whalers and Reindeer Herders of Northern Eurasia,** Hanover and London, University Press of New England.

Kulonen, Ulla-Maija, Seurujärvi-Kari, Irja, Pulkkinen, Risto, 2005. **The Saami, A Cultural Encyclopaedia,** Suomalaisen Kirjolliosuuden Seura.

Kuokkanen, Rauna, 2000. **Towards an 'Indigenous Paradigm' from a Sami Perspective**, In Canadian Journal of Native Studies p. 411–436.

Kuokkanen. Rauna, 2009. **Boares dego eana, Eamiálbmogiid diehtu, filosofiijat ja dutkan**, Čálliid Lágádus, Norge.

Kuoljok Eidlitz, Kerstin, 1999, **Moder jord och andra mödrar, Föreställningar om verkligheten bland folken i norr och vår syn på den**, Carlssons bokforl. Stockholm.

Kuoljok Eidlitz, Kerstin, 2009. **Bilden av universum bland folken i norr**, Carlssons bokforl. Stockholm.

Kuoljok, Apmut Ivar, Kuoljok John, Westman Kuhmunen, Anna. 2010. **Sejtar som har förts bort och kommit hem.** Småskrift / Ájtte Musei Vänner, Jokkmokk.

Lawson, E. T. and McCauley, R. N., 1990. **Rethinking Religion: Connecting Cognition and Culture.** Cambridge University Press.

Lehtola, Veli-Pekka, 2004. **The Sámi Peoples, Traditions in Transition**, ed. KustannusPuntsi Inari.

Lindmark, Daniel, 2004. Den ädle vilden och den okristlige svensken, in: ed. Lantto, Patrik, Sköld, Peter (red) **Befolkning och bosättning i norr: etnicitet, identitet och gränser i historiens sken**, Umeå: Centrum för samisk forskning, Umeå universitet, 2004 p. 127–154.

MacGuire, Meredith B. 2008. **Lived Religion. Lived ReligionFaith and Practice in Everyday Life.** Oxford University Press.

Magga Ole Henrik, Oskal Nils, Sara Mikkel Nils, 2001. **Dyrevelferd i samisk kultur,** report to the Norwegian Ministry of Agriculture and Food on 19.11.2001.

Magga, Ole Henrik, 2011. **Samisk natursyn, Speech at conference with the Friends of the Earth 22.01.2011,** website www.naturvernforbund.no downloaded on 08.05.2013.

Manker, Ernst, 1965. **Nåidkonst, Trolltrummans bildvärld,** Lt Forlag Sverige.

Mathisen, Stein Roar, 2004. **Hegemonic representations of Sámi culture: from narratives of noble savages to discourses on ecological Sámi.** In: Siikala, Anna-Leena, Klein Barbro & Mathisen Stein R. (eds.), 2004. Creating Diversities. Folklore, Religion and the Politics of Heritage. Studia Fennica Folkloristica 14 Helsinki, p. 17–30.

Mebius, Hans, 2007. Bissie - Studier i samisk religionshistoria, Östersund Sweden.

Miller, Barbara, 2007. Connecting and Correcting, A Case Study of Sámi Healers in Porsanger, CNWS Leiden.

Myrhaug, May-Lisbeth, 1997. I Modergudinnens fotspor. Sámisk religion med vekt på kvinnelige kulturutøvere og gudinnekult, Pax forlag Oslo.

Myrvoll, Marit, 1999. Å Skape en ny orden, bidrag i "Vi bekjenner at jorden hører Herren til, Studieprosjekt i Sápmi, Den Norske Kirke Samisk Kirkeråd, 1996–1999, p. 27–29.

Myrvoll, Marit, 2000, De underjordiske tåla icke korstegnet...- om tro og råd mot de underjordiske, Bårjås p. 50–58.

Myrvoll, Marit, 2010. «Bare gudsordet duger» Om kontinuitet og brudd i sámisk virkelighetsforståelse, Avhandling levert for graden Philosophia doctor, Universitet i Tromsø.

Natvig, Richard, 2006. Religionsvitenskapelig feltarbeid, i Kraft, Siv Ellen, Natvig, Richard Methode i religionsvitenskap, Pax forlag Oslo, p. 203–221.

Nergård, Jens – Ivar, 2006. Den levende erfaring, en studie i samisk kunnskapstradisjon, Cappelen Oslo.

Nurit Bird-David, 2002. 'Animism' revisited: Personhood, environment, and relational epistemology, in Harvey Graham (ed.), 2002, Readings in Indigenous Religions, Continuum New York, p. 319–342.

Oskal, Nils A, 1995. Det rette, det gode og reinlykken, avhandling til Dr. Art. graden i filosofi, Institutt for Samfuinnsvitenskap Universitetet i Tromsø.

Outakoski, Nilla Aimo Antti, 1991. Lars Levi Laestadiuksen saarnojen maahiskuva: Verrattuna Kaaresuvannon nomadien maahiskäsityksiin (Underground Spirits in the Sermons of Lars Levi Laestadius and Lappish Folklore), Acta Societatis Historicae Ouluensis, Scripta historica XVII.

Paltto, Kirste, 2012. The White Stone, (Vilges Geaðgi), Davvi girji, Karasjok.

Paulson, Ivar, 1961. Wildgeister im Volksglauben der Lappen, in Zeitschrift für Ethnologie, Bd 86, H 1, p. 141–151.

Pentikäinen, J, 1997. Die Mythologie der Saamen, Reinhold Schletzer Verlag, Berlin.

Pentikäinen, Juha (Ed), 2000. Sámi folkloristics, Turku.

Porsanger, Jelena, 2004. An essay about indigenous methodology, in: **Nordlit 15, Special issue on Northern Minorities,** Working papers of the University of Tromsø, p. 105–120.

Porsanger, Jelena, 2007. **Bassejoga cáhci":** Gáldut nuortasámiid eamioskkoldaga birra álgoálbmotmetodologiijaid olis / **The Water of the Sacred River: The Sources of the** Indigenous Religion of the Eastern Sami Examined Within the Framework of Indigenous Methodologies, **Davvi Girji, Karasjok Norway.**

Porsanger, Jelena, 2011. **Sámi Concepts and Modern Indigenous Approaches to Theorizing Their Culture** p. 59–69.

Porsanger, Jelena, 2012. Indigenous Sámi Religion: General Considerations about Relationship, in **The diversity of sacred lands in Europe: proceedings of the third Workshop of the Delos Initiative Inari/Aanaar, Finland, 1–3 July 2010,** edited by JoseMaria Mallarach, Thymio Papayannis and Rauno Väisänen p. 37–57.

Pyyssiäinen, Illka, 2004. Folk religion and theological correctness. I. Temenos Nordic Journal of Comparative religion. Vol 39–40 (2003–2004) p. 151–165.

Qvigstad J., 1920. **Lappischer Aberglaube,** Etnografisk Museum. Kristiania.

Qvigstad, J., 1926. **Lappiske Eventyr og Sagn (Bind I) fra Varanger,** Aschehoug Oslo.

Qvigstad, J., 1928. **Lappiske Eventyr og Sagn (Bind II) fra Troms og Finnmark,** Aschehoug Oslo.

Qvigstad, J., 1929. Lappiske Eventyr **og Sagn (Bind IV) fra Lyngen 2 og fra Nordland,** Aschehoug Oslo.

Rappaport, Roy A., 1975. **Pigs for the Ancestors,** Yale University Press.

Rappaport, Roy A., 1999. **Ritual and Religion in the Making of Humanity,** Cambridge.

Rautio, Anna-Maria, Josefsson Torbjörn, Axelsson, Anna-Lena, Östlund Lars 2015. **People and Pines 1555–1910: integrating ecology, history and archeology to assess long-term resource use in northern Fennoscandia.** Research article in Landscape Ecology, Springer. Online edition, first published 28. July 2015, p. 1–13.

Ravila, Paave, 1934. **Reste Lappischen Volksglaubens,** Mémoires de la Société Finnoougrienne, Helsinki.

Renvall- Helander, Elina, 2010. Animism, personhood and the nature of reality: Sami perspectives. In Polar record 46 (2010) p 44–56.

Rønnow Tarjei 2007. Tradisjoner i endring: religion som miljøvern og miljøvern som religion. In: Sigurd Hjelde and Otto Krogseth (red.) Religion – et vestlig fenomen? Oslo: Gyldendal akademisk p. 79–97.

Ryd, Yngve, 2007. Ren och Varg Samer berättar, Natur & Kultur forlag Stockholm.

Rydving, Håkan O. 1993. Samisk religionshistorisk bibliografi. Almqvist & Wiksell International.

Rydving, Håkan O., 1993. The End of Drum-Time, Religious Change Among the Lule Sámi 1670s–1740s, Uppsala Universitet.

Rydving, Håkan O., 1995. Samisk religionshistoria, Några källkritiska problem, Uppsala Universitet.

Rydving, Håkan O., 2004. Saami religion and Saami folk religion. What is the difference? Temenos 2004 Volum 39–40, p. 143–149.

Rydving, Håkan O., 2004. The End of Drum-Time: bakgrund, metodproblem och tillbakablick. Institutionen för genus, historia, litteratur och religion, Södertörns högskola.

Rydving, Håkan O., 2010. The "Bear Ceremonial" and Bear Rituals among the Khanty and the Sami, in Temenos Vol. 46 No 1 (2010) p. 31–52.

Rydving, Håkan O., 2010. Tracing Sami Traditions, in Search of the Indigenous Religion among the Western Sami during the 17th and 18th Centuries, Novus forlag Oslo.

Sámi Instituhtta, 2008. Ethics in Sámi and Indigenous Research, Dieđut 2008/1, Karasjok Norge.

Samisk Kirkeråd 1999. Rapport "Vi bekjenner at jorden hører Herren til" Studieprosjekt Sápmi 1994–1996 Den Norske Kirken.

Schanche, Audhild, 2002. Meahcci, den samiske utmarka, I Dieđut 2002–1, Sámi Instituhta Kautokeino, p. 156–170.

Segal, Robert A., 2012. Religon As Ritual – Roy Rappaports Changing Views from Pigs for the Ancestors (1968) to Rituals in the Making of Humanity (1999) in Stausberg, M (ed), 2012 Contemporary Theories of Religion A Critical Compagnon, Routledge p. 66–82.

Solbakk, Age, Solbakk, Mihkku, 2006. Bálvvosbáikkit ja noaiddesvuohta Deatnogáttis, Čálliid Lágádus, Tana, Norge.

Solbakk, Age, 2009. What We Believe In. Čálliid Lágádus, Norway.

Stausberg, Michael (ed), 2012. **Contemporary Theories of Religion A Critical Compagnon,** Routledge p. 66–82.

Sveen, Arvid, 2003. **Mytisk Landskap,** Orkana Forlag.

Tafjord, Bjørn Ola. **Indigenous Religion(s) as an Analytical Category.** In: Method & Theory in the Study of Religion, v25 n3 (2013): p. 221–243.

Tahuwai Smith, Linda, 1999/2012. **Decolonizing methodologies, research and indigenous peoples,** Zed books ltd. London.

Tandberg, Håkon, 2013. **Fra Gud via symbol til overmennesklig agent,** in: Tidsskrift for religion og kultur DIN, 1/2013, p. 7–31.

Taylor, Bron, 2010. **Dark Green Religion: Nature Spirituality And The Planetary Future,** University of California Press.

Tillhagen Carl-Hermann, 1969. Finnen und Lappen als Zauberkündige in der skandinavischen Volksüberlieferung, **in Kontakte und Grenzen, Festschrift G. Heilfurth** p. 129–43, Göttingen.

Turi, Johan, 2010. **Muitalus Sámiid birra,** Čálliid Lágádus, Kárásjohká Norway.

Turi, Johan, 2012. **An Account of the Sámi,** Čálliid Lágádus, Karasjok Norway.

Turi, Johan, Turi, Per, with the cooperation of K.B. Wiklund ed. By Emilie Demant-Hatt, 1920. **Lappish texts** D. Kgl. Danske Vidensk. Selsk. Skifter 7, København.

Vorren, Ørnulv, Eriksen, Hans Kr., 1993. **Sámiske offerplasser i Varanger,** Nordkalott forlag. United Nations Secretariat of the Permanent Forum on Indigenous Peoples' Issues, 2008. **Resource Kit on Indigenous Poeples' Issues.** United Nations, New York.

Verschuuren Bas, Wild, Robert, Mc Neeley Jeffrey, Oviedo Gonzalo 2010. Sacred **Natural Sites, Conserving Nature and Culture,** International Union for the Conversation of Nature.

Willerslev, Rane, 2007, **Soul Hunters, Hunting, Animism and Personhood Among the Siberian Yukaghirs,** University of California Press.

World Commission on Environment and Development (WCED), 1987. **Our Common Future.** Oxford: Oxford University Press.

Wu, Jianguo, 2013. **Landscape sustainability science: ecosystem services and human well-being in changing landscapes.** Research arcticle in Landscape Ecology (2013), 28: 999–1023. Springer.

References to the introduction

Geertz, C. 1993a [1973]. The interpretation of cultures: selected essays. London: Fontana.

Hastrup, K. 1990. Island of anthropology: studies in past and present Iceland. Odense: Odense University Press.

Ingold, T. 2000. The perception of the environment: essays on livelihood, dwelling and skill. London: Routledge.

Latour, B. 1993. We have never been modern. New York: Harvester Wheatsheaf.

Turner, F. 1986. "Reflexivity as Evolution in Thoreau's Walden" in: The Anthropology of experience. V. W. Turner and E. M. Bruner (red), pp. 39. Urbana and Chicago: University of Illinois Press.

Appendix to Chapter 4: Schematic Overview of Species-Related Protection Spirits

X = one story or mention of the name is recorded, NX = number of stories known.

Names of *máddo* in Sámi if available in the source.

Animal species	Qvigstad	Turi	Itkonen	Kalstad	Andersen	Div	MB Field work
Squid	3X II: 1928: 477 *skut'tarmad'doII*, 1928: 726 (2 historier)				5X 2005: 72, 73 *akkarmáddo*		
Lobster					X 2005: 73 *hummermáddo*		
Haddock						X Saba *hysens opphav*	
Red fish				3X 1997: 25 *háhkamáddo*	3X 2005: 73 *háhkamáddo*		
Pike			X*maddu* 1946: 105				
Trout			X*maddu* 1946: 105				
Lake whitefish			X*maddu* 1946: 105				
Other lake fish							X NN p. 86 *máddo*
"The fish"	X II, 1928: 478 *guol'le mad'do*				X Andersen 2005: 72 *guollemáddo*		

Animal species	Qvigstad	Turi	Itkonen	Kalstad	Andersen	Div	MB field work
Squirrel							X ST *máddo*
Lemen				X 1997: 25 *luomekmáddo*			
Mouse	X II, 1928: 477						X AB Máddo
Fox				X 1997: 25 *riebjimáddo*			
Wolf						X Fellman	
Beaver						X Fellman	
Otter	X I, 1927: 549 Čæw'ra-mad'do				X 2005: 71		
Bear						X Fellman	
General						Oskal 1995:96 *máddu.*	
All animals have a *máddo*	2X I, 1927:416; II, 192 8:474	X			X 2005: 72		X (SP; ST)

Animal species	Qvigstad	Turi	Itkonen	Kalstad	Andersen	Div	MB fieldwork
Mosquito		X 1920: 217 čuoika ädni					
Dung beetle	X II 1928: 474 *ruow'de garanas mad'do*						
Ant				X1997: 2 *gårkkomáddo*	X 2005: 71 *gårgåmáddo*		
Frog	9X I. 1927: 416–417; I 1927: 549II, 1928: 475 *Cubbom addo* II, 1928: 477 *Stuora cubbo* II, 1928: 725 (tre historier: *eadni/ maddo*) IV, 1929:329331 mad'do (2 historier)	2X 2011:127 192 0:217 *cubboeatni*	2X 1946: 10 6 *tšubbomaddu*	X 1997: 25	X 2005: 71 *tsuobbomáddo*		
Sand Lizard	X II, 1928: 725 dæžže-lággis mad'do						
Snow Grouse							X app.
Mother of the birds		X eatni					

Other Collected Máddo Stories

About Nils Jernsletten after the Snow Grouse Hunt

In her introduction to a lecture by Professor Jens-Ivar Nergård in the public library in Tromsø on 17 April 2013 where I was present, Professor Synnøve des Bouvrie from Tromsø University told the audience a *máddo* story that Nils Jernsletten (1934–2012), professor of the Sámi language, had told her some time before 1984. Nils Jernsletten was from Tana in Eastern Finnmark. He had just returned from snow-grouse hunting over the weekend. They sat in the university cafeteria when he told her that one should not over-hunt because then a large snow grouse – "stor rypa" was the Norwegian term he used – could come and punish him.

He was told this story as a child and he could still feel the fear of the "stor rypa" as a physical pressure on his shoulders and chest. (Story published with permission of the author.)

Asta Balto Afraid of Mouse *Máddo*

This story was told in April 2013 by Asta Balto (b. circa 1950, she grew up in Karasjok), an expert in Sámi education and teaching at the Sámi high school in Kautokeino. Asta explained that when she was a child a group of children had been playing with mice. They had put them in a metal pan and the mice were bloodying their claws and were very anxious to escape. It is usual that Sámi children play for long intervals unattended by adults. Afterward, when her mother heard about this, she scared her by stating that the children should never torment mice in this way again, otherwise the mouse *máddo* might come and punish them. Asta was very afraid of the *máddo* then, but she told me the story with a twinkle in her eye. (Story published with permission of the author.)

Solveig Tangeraas' *Máddo* Stories
Told in May 2013 in Indre Billefjord, Porsanger, West-Finmark

Solveig Tangeraas is active in the local Sámi association, born circa 1940, grew up and still lives in Billefjord/Porsanger and one of the key informants of my research. She told me two *máddo* stories, one from her childhood and one from her adult life. As a child she was together with another girl on their daily walk to the school bus when two small animals with large tails suddenly jumped onto the road and stood motionless there. The girls did not dare walk any further on the road so as not to chase the unknown animals away. The girls were convinced that any disturbance could provoke the *máddo* of that animal. They returned home. Solveig's mother had to take the boat to bring them to school, as they were too late for the school bus. Later she realized the unknown animals had been a squirrel. They were unusual in the area at that time. (Story recorded by M. B. Feb. 2013.)

The second *máddo* story concerned the frogs in their well. When they had to remove and rebuild the well, her husband (who was not from a Sámi area and did not have the same traditional upbringing as she) insisted that they remove the frogs living in the well. They brought them carefully to another place. When the well was redone, they had dirty water for many weeks. The new cover of the well turned out to be leaky. Solveig believed that this was the revenge of the frog *máddo* for having removed the frogs. Frogs were very frequent in those times and were necessary in a drinking well so as to keep the water free of insects, plants and all other foreign bodies.

Appendix to Chapter 5

Asking Permission of the Underground People When Building the Sámi High School

Translation of the Norwegian Broadcasting Company (NRK) article

May Brit Utsi was rector at the Sámi high school when the building project started and she is of the opinion that everything was done the right way. Before one starts the building process, it is ancient Sámi tradition to ask the underground people for permission. That we did, says Utsi, and when the state building company came and wished to start constructing the Diehtosiida, she put up a lavvo on the building site. She spent the night together with some employees of the state building company.

"We cooked meat and had several ceremonies that are usual in relationship to Sámi custom and superstition. Among other things we put the bone scraps outside on the ground after having eaten the meat so as to please the underground spirits. Using sticks, we made three squares outside the lavvo and recited certain incantations that are usual in Sámi popular belief."

When they awoke the next morning they had had a good night's sleep without any disturbance and found a black spider in one of the squares. This was interpreted as a positive sign, and construction could proceed.

"Mai Britt Utsi var rektor ved Samisk høgskole da byggeprosjektet startet og hun mener at ting ble gjort riktig. Før man setter i gang med en bygge-prosess er det ifølge gammel samisk tradisjon vanlig å spørre om lov av de underjordiske, og det gjorde vi, sier Utsi. Hun forteller at da Statsbygg kom til Kautokeino og skulle starte byggingen av Diehtosiida, satt hun opp en lavvo på bygge-tomta. Der overnattet hun sammen med de ansatte i Statsbygg. Vi kokte kjøtt og hadde diverse seremonier som er vanlig i forhold til sámisk skikk og overtro. Blant annet satt vi ut beinrestene etter at vi hadde spist kjøttet, dette for å blidgjøre de underjordiske. Vi laget også tre firkanter av vedstokkker utenfor lavvoen og så leste vi opp formularer som er vanlig i forhold til samisk overtro, sier Utsi" (http://www.nrk.no/kanal/nrk_sapmi/ 1.7398832 lastet ned 2 May 2013).

Appendix to Chapter 7

Schema of Gods and Goddesses in Some Key Missionary Accounts

Accounts from Skanke, Jessen-Schardebøll, Anonymous at Leem, Sidenius Forbus, Sigvard Kildal, analyzed by Rydving (1995) and added are some remarks of Itkonen (1946).

The names of the divinities are written in the way they figure in the sources quoted. For the remainder of the text the contemporary standard spelling of Northern Sámi is used.

Placement	Name and properties of the divinity	Offerings, rituals and symbols
Gods and goddesses high in the starry heavens	*Radien, Zhioaarve- radien,* highest god in the starry heavens, the "horn god" who takes care of reindeer, is another name or aspect of *Radien. Radienkjedde* is his son (Rydving 1995: 78–79, 125, 128). *Radienkjedde* has the power to shape and maintain "all things," also soul and spirit (Skanke quoted in Rydving 1995: 128). Rules over all other gods. Takes souls back if they are obedient to the gods and are therefore released from *jabaime* (Rydving 1995: 80, 126).	*Radien atsie*: main offering-tree and symbol, is a *wærro-mourra*, blood-tree; the tree was smeared with blood; his symbol is a cross. Offerings are elk or *sarva*: male reindeer (Rydving 1995: 125, 12).
	Wife of *Radien: Sergve-edni* (Skanke synops 2: 7). Shapes human soul, sends it to *maderakka* (*Rydving* 1995: 128).	

Placement	Name and properties of the divinity	Offerings, rituals and symbols
	Ruona-nieid (Rydving 1995: 81), lives not far from Radien; makes the grass green in the spring and gives new grass to the reindeer.	Spinning wheel. Offerings at springtime.
God and goddesses in the heavens	*Maderatja* fetches the souls from *Radien achhie/ Radienkjedde* and sends them to the *maderatja*, who sends them down on sun rays to earth, to *maderakka*, who puts them in the womb. The son of the sun is the mythological ancestor of the Sámi. *Bieive/* sun or *beive nieida/*daughter. *Beive nieida* warms the earth and makes everything grow (Rydving 1995: 81–82, 128).	*Beive*: white male animals, a white goat is sacrificed at midsummer and porridge eaten, a ring of grass hung up (Rydving 1995: 81–2, 132). Also spinning wheel, flax-plant (Rydving 1995: 159). At the reappearance of the sun after the dark time was celebrated, and at every sunrise the Skolt Sámi bowed to the sun, and at sunset they said "God is not visible anymore," according to J. Fellman (quoted in Itkonen 1946: 8). In the morning the sun rode on a bear, at midday on a male reindeer, and in the evening on a female reindeer, an "aldu," according to a Skolt Sámi myth, quoted in Itkonen (1946: 8).

Placement	Name and properties of the divinity	Offerings, rituals and symbols
	Maderatja and *Maderakka* live in the middle parts of the air. *Mader-adja*, "the highest or the airy regions that give fertility and movement to all living things" (Rydving 1995: 128). Skanke and Anonymous at Leem have different perspectives as to whom defines sex (*Maderakka* or *Juksakka*) and forms the body (*Maderakka* or *Sarakka*). *Maderakku*, the mid-level airy regions: "Saa syvnes deres gamle Noider ligesaa at have holdt Luften for et Guddoms vesen, som de hâr kaldet *Maderakka*, og skulle være *Maderatjas* kone" (quoted by Rydving 1995: 133). (Skanke synopsis 2: 46) Puts souls in the womb and shapes the body; is for female health and the reproduction of humans and animals (Skanke 1995: 128–9) and *Maderatja* stands above the sun on drums (Skanke synops pp. 133–135).	*Maderatja* is symbolized as a circle, triangle orsixangle on drums (Rydving 1995: 127.)
	Horagallis: thunder god, can hurt, scare or disperse reindeer (Hans Skanke 1995 quoted in Rydving: 133).	Uncastrated male animals, not of black color. No women can be present at offerings (Skanke quoted by Rydving 1995: 158–159).
	Gisen-olmai / wind and weather god; *Mannu*/Moon; *Ailegas* / gods of the three holy days Friday, Saturday, Sunday; *Biegolmai* / wind god and also god of the oceans and other bodies of water.	

Placement	Name and properties of the divinity	Offerings, rituals and symbols
Gods and goddesses in the lower skies / on earth	*Leib-olmai* / forest and hunting god who responsible for the upbringing of boys; *Kiöse olmai,* fishing god; the four *áhkkus* – responsible for the reproduction of animals and humans. *Maderakka*'s three daughters: *Sarakka* (at the lowest level of air, according to Skanke synopsis 2: 46): "Ti æres og dyrkes Hun fremfor alle de andre" Rydving 1995: 135) and takes care of girls; *Uksakka* (door goddess, birth goddess who protects newborns); and *Juksakka* (changes girls to boys in the womb). According to Anonymous in Leem, it is *Sarakka* who gives a body to babies in the womb (Rydving 1995: 94).	*Sarakka:* honor with every item of food or drink, water or brandy and porridge, mostly without drum. Cock and hens, reindeer calves, female dogs, offerings made by women only. Children are baptized in her name. Lives in the fireplace (Rydving 1995: 130, 136).
	Maderakka, Uksakka and *Sarakka* give bodies and fertility to both humans and animals. *Saivo olmai, saiwo*-animals (Rydving 1995: 129). Fellman says *mader akku* is under the earth (quoted in Itkonen 1946: 10).	
Gods and goddesses a short ways under the earth.	*Jabme-akku,* mother of death (Rydving 1993: 112–113).	Offering to stay alive.
Gods and goddesses deep in the earth.	*Rota.* God of sickness (Rydving 1993: 114–117).	Dead horses, sledges, pine tree twigs and tops, special sacrifice places where no other gods are sacrificed to (S. Kildal quoted in Rydving 1995 p. 116, Rydving 1993: 114–117).

Band   20   Mardoeke Boekraad: Ecological Sustainability in Traditional Sámi Beliefs and Rituals.
2016.

www.peterlang.com